LANZAROTE

Raimundo Rodríguez

Title: LANZAROTE
Writing and coordination: Raimundo Rodríguez
Collaboration: Manuel Ramírez
             Rosa Guerrero
             Javier Cuadrado
             Nona Perera
             José Manuel Onieva
             Antonio Tovar
             Rafael Paredes
Photography: Raimundo Rodríguez
             Blas Gil Rodríguez (guirre)
             Grafcán (aerial photography)
Illustrations: José Alfonso Madrid
Translations: German: Martin Kreutzer
             English: Manolita Pérez
Photo Editing and Layout: Raimundo Rodríguez
Color Separations, Printing and Binding: Tecnographic S.L. Seville
First Edition: January 1998
Registered Number: SE - 2028/97
I.S.B.N.: 84-922057-7-6
Publisher and Distribution: Guías y Mapas **RAI•MUNDO**
             - Urbanization Jundía Mar H-81
               Moro Jable. FUERTEVENTURA
               Tl.: 928 - 54 25 50
             - C/ San Miguel, 8. 3º Dcha.
               41002 SEVILLA
               Tl.: 95 - 437 30 38

CONTENTS

Geological Origin   6

Insular structure.   12
    Mountains. Volcanoes. Malpaises. Plains. Jables. Coasts. Agriculture. Singular Points.

Natural Resources.   16
    Climate (16). Habitation and Insular Evolution (16). Flora (17). Fauna (21). Fishing (23).
    Hunting (29).

Protected Natural Areas.   30
    Timanfaya National Park (31). Archipelago of Chinijo Natural Park (37).
    Integral Natural Reserve of the Islets (42). Natural Park of the Volcanoes(42).
    La Corona Nature Monument (44). Los Ajaches Nature Monument (46).
    La Cueva de Los Naturalistas Nature Monument (46).
    Nature Monument of Islote de Halcones (47). Nature Monument of Las Montañas del Fuego (48).
    Tenegüime Protected Landscape (48). La Geria Protected Landscape (49).
    Place of Scientific Interest of Los Jameos (50). Place of Scientific Interest of Janubio (51).

History and Culture.   52
    Prehistory (52). The Conquest (54). Modern History (55). Socio-political Structure (61).
    Economy (61). Customs (64). Festivities (66). Traditional Games (68). Arts and Crafts (69).

Island Architecture.   70
    Old Architecture (70).
      Religious edification: Churches, Hermitages, and Convents (70).
      Unique buildings: Cemeteries, Fortifications, Lighthouses, Cillas, Taros and Marettas (71).
      Industrial Archaeology: Tanneries, Tahonas, Mills, Molinas, Lime Ovens and Salt flats (75).
      Residential Construction: Popular Housing and Lordly Housing (78).
    Contemporaneous Architecture (80).
      César Manrique: life and works (80). Jameos del Agua (82).
      Monument to the Peasant (83). Garden of Cactus (85).

Practical Information.   86
    Visas (86). Customs (86). Currency (87). Tourist Information (90). Communications (90).
    Health (91). Accommodation (92). Rental Car y Bicycles (92). Sports (93). Gastronomy (94).

Places.   96
    Arrecife (96). **Haría** (99). **Teguise** (101). **San Bartolomé** (108). **Tinajo** (110). **Tías** (112).
    Yaiza (114). History. General Information. Patrimony. Surroundings. Points of Interest.

Beaches.   116
    Reducto, Bastián, Cucharas, Caletón Blanco, Risco, Famara, Santa Sport,
    Mujeres, Pozo, Cera, Papagayo, Caleta del Congrio, Puerto Muelas,
    Blanca, Pocillos and Las Conchas.

Bibliography and Maps   123

AUTHOR'S NOTE

This is my second work on the Canary islands. With the experience and the knowledge accumulated previously, I have wanted to learn more of this place that is so peculiar to the earth. All the topics have been treated with enough rigor so that the reader can notice the importance that these islands have at the geologic, biological, and historical levels. At the moment this island is one of the more important tourist destinations in Europe. This brings up a delicate situation: the high level of produced deterioration and the universal necessity of the conservation of the island's values. I think that this need to conserve, not only in Lanzarote but for the rest of the world should not be enforced. The prohibition would generate the demand for rights: the norms of uses and behaviors in certain areas give too much freedom for the destruction of non-protected areas.

The education and a certain level of assimilated information in an interesting way gives place the knowledge and the respect of our environment. All surroundings change when we know how to observe their qualities. When we think on the formation of the continents and all beings throughout time, we will understand our position in the evolutionary process and the little right we have to modify it. We should thank our ancestors. When we observe their works, we can think about how their efforts allowed them to achieve a good end. Adding to this is their acquired wisdom during hundreds of fruitful years of observation and their system of communication from generation to generation. And a way to thank them is by protecting and restoring their legacy.

Mainly I want to dedicate this research work to all those people that have helped to preserve the tradition behind the scenes with their silent but constant work; it is because of them that we can learn from the past. They are also the people that on occasion we include in pictures as part of the landscape. Unfortunately they are the last representatives of an already forgotten model of life. And also, to those who have dedicated their time to teach me, I thank them for the knowledge I have received.

At the same time I want to name my recently born daughter, Sara. She has given me the last « push « to finish this troublesome, although gratifying work.

I hope everyone who reads this book is touched by the feeling with which it was made and among all help to make this a better world.

Raimundo Rodríguez

INTRODUCTION

A visit to Lanzarote is always an unforgettable experience. If you want to enjoy your stay on the Island, this book can serve as a very useful guide. Inside these pages you will find information about changing foreign currencies, health centers, transportation, lodgings, diving and windsurfing clubs, and many other services that you may require on your visit. But there is something more offered on this island that is not included in the above list of services. It is written by a traveller so the book can be a companion for you on your trip. This book gives you the opportunity to fully enjoy and discover the treasures of a magical island.

Some of these treasures take us to the time in which the first humans swarmed around the oriental Africa. Also to the fields of dunes of Lanzarote from about 6 million years ago, in which one of the biggest non-flying birds and big terrestrial turtles of more than a meter long have ever existed on Earth. Others connect us with the people who were the first to colonize an Island and didn't know any other human beings. And they called this island, *Tyterogaka*. Some towns settled in the Canary Islands for more than two millenniums until, in 1402, a small army under control of the Norman, Jean of Bethencourt and Gadifer de la Salle, arrived in *Tyterogaka*. After the conquest, the Island was added to the Kingdom of Castile. It is at this moment that the History of Lanzarote and The Canary's begin.

It is a history of Berberisc pirates attacks, whose legends impregnate the walls of the fortifications and the reconstructed temples after the lootings. It is a history that has always been dependent upon the volcano that, between 1730 and 1736, gave place to an incredible eruptive episode. It was one of the biggest eruptions that man has ever witnessed and ruined part of the Island in the process. At the same time it created new options for living. *Timanfaya* arose as a pristine and untouched landscape. The volcano suggests to us the paradox of a space born from the womb of the earth and which can take us to other worlds. A history characterized by cycles of mono-agricultural export, which like the cochineal, has a quick rate of expansion. And sooner or later, after the market crashes, there is a sharp crisis and emigration occurs.

The peasants of Lanzarote were conditioned by the volcano, by the wind, and by the drought. The *conejeros* (people from the island) adapted to the hardness of the conditions of life on the Island. They used their genius to develop original ways to take advantage of the scarce resources. They created landscapes of a singular beauty, cultivating in enarenados or in the *jable* and, especially, in the prodigious garden of *La Geria*. On the coast, they built gardens of salt by molding the mud with lime and stone. They were evolving to make more efficient use of the sun, the wind and the tides. They occupied the coast using it as a resting place and big travellers' inn. Every winter, these inns are over crowded due to extended vacations.

The vineyards of *La Geria*, the salt flats, the lime ovens, the mills and *molinas*, the temples and fortifications, the seigniorial constructions and the houses of the *conejeros*, the coast, the wind, and the volcano. These were the vital references of an universal *conejero* whose life and works are fundamental in understanding the actual Lanzarote.

César Manrique was born in Lanzarote in 1920. This Canary artist worked as a painter and sculptor, developing an architectural art that integrated the given resources with an exquisite sensibility. César was one of the first to support the conception of development models adapted to the nature of the Islands as well as a fighter for a better quality of life. His numerous works represent an ethics model and environmental aesthetics. In Lanzarote, the *Jameos del Agua*, the *Mirador del Río* or his house, which nowadays is the actual headquarters of the foundation which takes his name (in Tahiche), are specially famous. They conform an outstanding part of the patrimony of the Island along with the rest of his works.

I remember a conversation with César in which he told us that if El Golfo was an emerald, the *Salinas of Janubio* were the pearl of Lanzarote. Our conversation went from the intimate recognition of the beauty of the resources of the Island, to the concern for the future. In fact, this is the fundamental sense of this book. We are convinced that knowing the patrimony is the best guarantee for the preservation, in an Island that has been declared as a Reservation of the Biosphere by the UNESCO. It depends on us in large part that Lanzarote continues to conserve its treasures, which motivate this declaration and facilitate each visitor to have an unforgettable experience. If you have this spirit to travel to the Island, you will surely find multiple aspects of interest in the following pages.

Happy stay in Lanzarote.

Rafael Paredes

GEOLOGICAL ORIGIN

Lanzarote island belongs to the Canary Archipelago. It is a volcanic group situated in the center-oriental Atlantic, at the NW of the African Continent.

There are at present seven theories about the Archipelago formation. One of the most complex sustains the opinion that it was a combined process of underwater eruptions of lava and the thrusting up of large sections of oceanic crust. The detection of the African Plate had as a consequence the pressure of the Atlantic Plate. Later on, the flow of lava occurred through fissures with a dominant direction which determined the shape and structure of the islands (most evident in Tenerife, La Palma and El Hierro), the alignment of the islands (Fuerteventura and Lanzarote) and the general configuration of dikes.

The different conditions of pressure, temperature and tensions happening in the profundity levels of the oceanic floor, originated fissures in the superficial part. Therefore, emerging platforms, collapses, and mechanic friction were produced by abrupt differences of pressure, causing the violent emissions of incandescent masses.

Lanzarote has, therefore, a volcanic origin, a decisive factor for its geomorphology and later on for its successive inhabitants (animals and vegetable). Its geologic structure is the simplest and better studied of the archipelago. Among the islands, Lanzarote is the only island that has a sounding system that crosses the entire island structure. Thanks to Fúster and other researchers' works, the submarine structure, as well as the emerging area, are well known,.

The actual volcanic structure rests directly on oceanic sediments from the African continental bank (with micro-fauna from the Paleocene, with a depth of 2,598 meters. Tobas (sand stone) and submarine lava belonging to Oligocene (according with the micro-fauna) appear at 353 meters depth,. One may suppose that the uprising insular structure took place during this period, since it definitely emerged after a numerous of submarine thrusts.

As we will see farther on, the present island landscape is the result of constructive agents such as the volcanism, and destructive agents such as the erosion. The continuing action of these agents cause the establishment of a huge range of substrates which are later on occupied by vegetation, and according to the chemical quality of the materials which constitute the above mentioned subtracts.

The age of the materials from the island are measured by the volcanic cones which are dismantled, more or less, and covered with vegetation. As we will see, Lanzarote is an island with smooth and undulating soil interrupted frequently by high cones, notorious cliffs (intensive marine erosion), and deep ravines.

As a consequence, the entire island is a great volcanic construction constituted by successive eruptions on an unsteady platform. The line of fractures come from the cast materials (lava) with enough pressure to reach the surface (volcanism is fissured by nature). These fracture lines are NE -SW oriented.

In the same manner the islets appeared located in the north of Lanzarote. They emerged from the more extensive marine platform of the archipelago.

The volcanic activity has never been continuous. Different eruptive periods can be recognized and classified in series or what amounts to the same thing, volcanic cycles (see geomorphologic map).

Series I (Old Series or First Volcanic Cycle) was formed by very old basaltic defiles (Miocene-

Situation of the Canary Islands. Dominant structural guidelines.

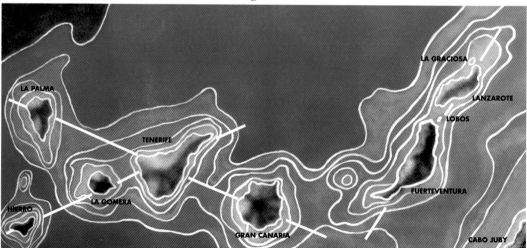

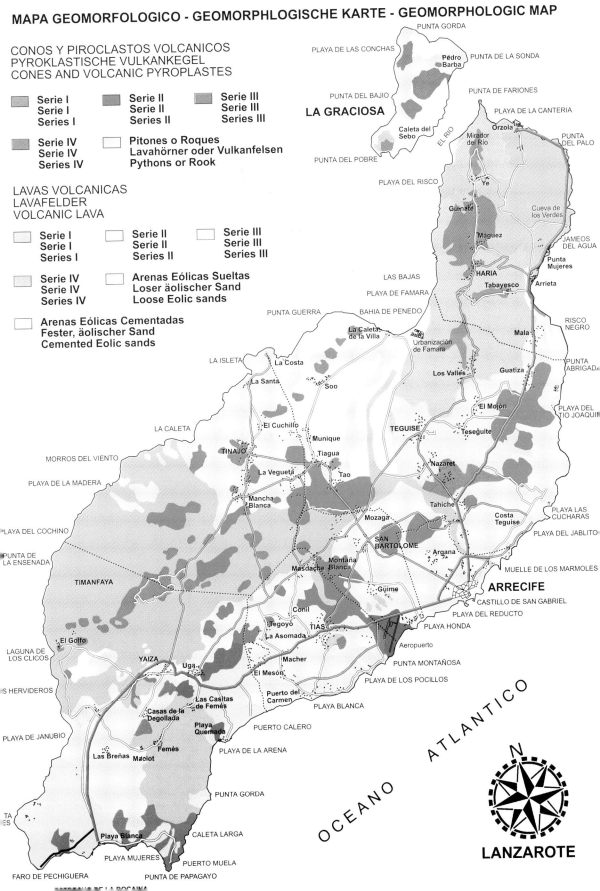

MAPA GEOMORFOLOGICO - GEOMORPHLOGISCHE KARTE - GEOMORPHOLOGIC MAP

CONOS Y PIROCLASTOS VOLCANICOS
PYROKLASTISCHE VULKANKEGEL
CONES AND VOLCANIC PYROPLASTES

Serie I
Serie I
Series I

Serie II
Serie II
Series II

Serie III
Serie III
Series III

Serie IV
Serie IV
Series IV

Pitones o Roques
Lavahörner oder Vulkanfelsen
Pythons or Rook

LAVAS VOLCANICAS
LAVAFELDER
VOLCANIC LAVA

Serie I
Serie I
Series I

Serie II
Serie II
Series II

Serie III
Serie III
Series III

Serie IV
Serie IV
Series IV

Arenas Eólicas Sueltas
Loser äolischer Sand
Loose Eolic sands

Arenas Eólicas Cementadas
Fester, äolischer Sand
Cemented Eolic sands

PUNTA GORDA
PLAYA DE LAS CONCHAS
Pedro Barba
PUNTA DE LA SONDA
PUNTA DEL BAJIO
PUNTA DE FARIONES
LA GRACIOSA
PLAYA DE LA CANTERIA
Órzola
Caleta del Sebo
EL RIO
Mirador del Río
PUNTA DEL PALO
PUNTA DEL POBRE
PLAYA DEL RISCO
Ye
Guinate
Cueva de los Verdes
JAMEOS DEL AGUA
Máguez
LAS BAJAS
HARIA
Punta Mujeres
Tabayesco
Arrieta
PLAYA DE FAMARA
PUNTA GUERRA
BAHIA DE PENEDO
RISCO NEGRO
La Caleta de la Villa
Urbanización de Famara
Mala
PUNTA ABRIGAD
LA ISLETA
La Costa
Los Vallés
Guatiza
La Santa
Soo
El Mojón
PLAYA DEL TIO JOAQUI
LA CALETA
El Cuchillo
TEGUISE
Teseguite
MORROS DEL VIENTO
Munique
TINAJO
Tiagua
Nazaret
PLAYA DE LA MADERA
La Vegueta
Tao
Tahiche
PLAYA LAS CUCHARAS
Mancha Blanca
Costa Teguise
PLAYA DEL COCHINO
Mozaga
PLAYA DEL JABLITO
PUNTA DE LA ENSENADA
SAN BARTOLOME
Argana
MUELLE DE LOS MARMOLES
TIMANFAYA
Masdache
Montaña Blanca
ARRECIFE
Güime
CASTILLO DE SAN GABRIEL
PLAYA DEL REDUCTO
Conil
El Golfo
Tegoyó
TIAS
PLAYA HONDA
LAGUNA DE LOS CLICOS
La Asomada
Aeropuerto
YAIZA
Macher
PUNTA MONTAÑOSA
Uga
El Mesón
PLAYA DE LOS POCILLOS
S HERVIDEROS
Puerto del Carmen
Las Casitas de Femés
PLAYA BLANCA
Casas de la Degollada
PLAYA DE JANUBIO
Playa Quemada
PUERTO CALERO
Femés
PLAYA DE LA ARENA
Las Breñas
Maciot
PUNTA GORDA
CALETA LARGA
OCEANO ATLANTICO
N
Playa Blanca
PLAYA MUJERES
PUERTO MUELA
FARO DE PECHIGUERA
PUNTA DE PAPAGAYO
LANZAROTE

Terciary Period), and remains at present, a reduced surface with 200 sq kilometres, spread out into two areas. These two areas (or shields) are *Famara* and Femés or *Los Ajaches* district. The latter formed mainly by an agglomeration of basaltic layers, which at the beginning might have been connected; as can be concluded by the existence of other nuclei of old substances in several areas of the island.

The *Famara* massif (cut in a length by a 500 meter high cliff) features all its constitution. Nevertheless, the Ajaches are much more weather-beaten.

The first effusive stage contains a period included between the -17 and 12 m.yrs-. After this, it appears again a few decades later by different mouths and alignments. The existence of plants and animals spread out through the soil among these eruptive periods

Series II and Series III constitute the so-called Second Volcanic Cycle (materials from the Pliocene-Pleistocene). They are characterised by volcanic formations of much less abrupt morphology like a strong limestone crust (plaster), covered sometimes by earthen soil which can be seen perfectly and recognized.

This Series was developed at the edge of the ancient shields mentioned earlier. In the south of *Famara* the uprisings correspond to the mountains of *Teneje, Chimia, San Rafael, Guanapay* and, to the north, *La Atalaya* de Haría. To the north of *Los Ajaches* we can see *Caldera Gritana, Tinasoria, La Montañeta, Montaña Riscada, Bermeja, Mojón*, etc…

Series III consists of biggest area of Lanzarote, spreading and covering part of the previous with very fluid basaltic uprisings, mainly in the centre of the island. The number of cones and calderas from this period is approximately 130, including the islets. The explosive phases of copious gasses and pyroclastic materials are combined with uprising phases of lava flow. The volcanoes of this period are better preserved.

The northern alignment is comprised of *Caldera Blanca, Montaña Tinajo, El Cuchillo*, the Soo Mountain grouping, *Tinamala*, as well as the group of *Calderetas* next to Guatiza, are notorious. Likewise *La Corona* Mountain, *Isaga, Tahiche* and the group of *Zonzamas* are worth mentioning. Further south in Series IV, the most outstanding alignment include: *Tinacho, Tizalaya* and *Tamia*. Running parallel with the leeward coast, the cones are more heterogeneous. The last alignment in the south, *Blanca* Mountain, *Guardilama* are joined together with the massif of *Los Ajaches*, and the *Atalaya de Femés* stand out.

Series IV or Recent Volcanism, from a few thousand years ago, includes the historic eruptions which formed the so-called "*Malpaises*" (pathless volcanic lava). These volcanoes are well preserved and

might have originated in recent history. Although we don't have historic references, like the NE-SW alignment of north of the island. These eruptions may have taken place between two thousand five hundred to three thousand years ago. *La Quemada* of Orzola, *La Corona, Helechos, Quemada*, and *Pescosa* volcanoes, as well as the *Peñas de Tao*, emerging from an enormous flood of lava. All these volcanoes constitute a perfect line of approximately 4 km. long.

The volcano of *La Corona* is the most important and it has as a main characteristic is a volcanic tuff 6.3 km. wide. This tuff gives rise to *Cueva de los Verdes* (a cave) and the other sixteen *jameos* (collapse of a tunnel roof) that appear along the track. This has a flow that carries through the *Malpaís de La Corona* (an area covered with lava in the eastern part of the island with 30 km. square area). In addition, this volcano has two arms or rivers of lava reaching the sea by going through *Risco de Famara* as well as the *Ginate* and *Rositas* valleys.

The historic eruptions of 1730, 1736 and the 1824 belong to the same series. They took place in well-known sectors like *Timanfaya* or *Montañas del Fuego* (mountains of fire). A big part in the west of the island is occupied by its lava, while the surrounding cones from the anterior series stayed isolated: the so-called *islotes* (islets). The area of constituted volcanoes and *Malpaises* extends over 200 sq km., from which 32 sq km. belong to the 1824 eruptions. There are about fifty cones lined up in this area.

The only references of the 1730 and 1736 eruptions came from the former priest of Yaiza, Mr. Andrés Lorenzo Curbelo and the Lanzarote Board. There are also references to the 1824 eruptions.

The Lanzarote historical eruptions correspond to:
- Area of Timanfaya: Sept. 1st 1730 to April 16th 1736.
- Tao eruption or called Clérigo Duarte: July 31st to October 16th 1824.
- Nuevo del Fuego Volcano: Sept. 29th to October 4th 1824.
- Tinguatón Volcano: October 16th to October 24th 1824.

The materials accumulated by the volcanoes are the basaltic (heavy black rocks). The sedimentary soil, which is of very little thickness, consists of sands and clay soil.

The sand moved by the wind current are constituted by small limestone grains and mollusc sea shells; these are thrown by the surge to the Soo sector, *Penedo* Bay, and to Orzola beaches. The winds make these sands (well-known as *Jables*) cross the island until the eastern coast.

The clay of aeolic origin are red soils that stem from The Sahara which the wind brings in as a dust cloud form. As a consequence, up to 2 kilograms by square meter per year of these sands are displaced,

GEOLOGIC TIME AND FORMATIONS. The geologists contain the history of the Earth in three eons:				
EON ARCHEOZOIC Ancient Times	The world already had some continental rock, an ocean, and an atmosphere. The life appears 3.500 m.yr ago in form of bacterias and algae.			4.600-2.500 m. yr.
PROTEROZOIC EON Era of the Primitive Life	The big continents and the extensive seas appeared. 1.800 m.yr. ago, the algae produced the enough oxygen as so they began to accumulate in the sea and in the atmosphere.			2.500-600 m. yr.
PHANEROZOIC EON Period of Geologic time of Visible Life (600 m. yr. until today) Complex life and modern forms. This Eon is divided in successive Eras according to those groups living in different times.	**Paleozoic or Primary Era** (600-248 m.yr.) The Eras are divided at the same time in periods:	**Cambrian**	All the life was limited to the water. It was, in general, warmer than the current time. The mountains began to grow and the volcanoes threw big plates of lava.	600-505 m.yr.
		Ordovician	Contraction of the oceans and appearance of the first continents. Trilobites lived, primitive corals, and many more invertebrates. Fishes appeared without jaw.	505-440 m.yr.
		Silurian	Marine silts produce rich reservations in petroleum. First plants and terrestrial animals.	440-408 m.yr.
		Devonian	Fossils found in the rocks from this period include river fishes and the first amphibians. The first forests also appear.	408-360 m.yr.
		Carboniferous	It takes the name from the coal strata which produces carbon. they are residuals of tropical forests. Norteamérica came into collision with South America and Europe with Africa. Great part of Antartic, Australia, South America, Africa, and India are covered by ice,.	360-286 m.yr.
		Permian	The union of the continents form great continents. The glaciers withdraw toward the south.	286-248 m.yr.
	Mesozoic or Secundary Period (248-65 m.yr.) The Era of the dinosaurs	**Triassic**	Fracture of the great continente. Big amphibians (1 m.), and advanced reptiles (1'5 m.).	248-213 m.yr.
		Jurassic	Warm climate. The primitive birds and mammals appear. Big herbivorous dinosaurs. The current continents have being formed	213-144 m.yr.
		Cretaceous	The deposits from this period include 60% of the reservations of petroleum known nowadays. The plants with flower and the big carnivorous dinosaurs appear. Massive death of dinosaurs and other creatures, perhaps for the impact of a great asteroid.	144-65 m.yr.

	Paleogene. (65-24'6 m.y.) The continents take their current form. The birds and the mammals occupied the Earth. It is divided at the same time in three Period:	**Paleocene**	65-55 m.yr.
Cenozoic or Terciary Period (65-2 m.yr.)		**Eocene**	55-38 m.yr.
		Oligocene	38-24'6 m.yr.
	Neogene. (24'6-2 m.a.) The crashing plates has been elevating the current mountainous chains. The movements of plates, the fault or the volcanic eruptions influenced in the formation of countless islands. **Formation of Canary Islands.**	**Miocene**	24'6-5 m.yr.
		Pliocene	5-2 m.yr.
Anthropic or Quaternary Era. (2 m.yr.- present time.) Repeated advances and setbacks of the ice. The last block of ice have melted since 10.000 year ago. The sea levels rise. The man developed. The fauna and the flora diminished.		**Pleistocene or Glacial Epoch**	2-0'01 m.yr.
		Holocene or Recent Epoch	10.000 years Present times.

contributing to the soil formation that later on will be used as farming area.

INSULAR STRUCTURE

Lanzarote is the most eastern island of the canary archipelago and the fourth in regards of extension, about 805 sq kilometres. There is a distance of 125 km. from Lanzarote to the African coast. At present, Lanzarote population is approximately 70.000 inhabitants.

Lanzarote is located in the Boreal Hemisphere between 13º 25' to 29º 20' North latitude. In the northern island are located a set of islets called *Chinijo* archipelago made of: La Graciosa, Alegranza, Monta-ña Clara, Roque del Este, and Roque del Oeste islets. Between Lanzarote and Fuerteventura Islands lies the strait of Bocaina with a minimum width of 10 km. and an average depth of 35-40 m.

Beside the natural environment elements and the geologic evolution process, the landscape of Lanzarote is determined by the environmental elements modified from men activities, such as farming style. All of that conditioned by a sub-desert climate environment.

First of all, we are going to define the landscape with geologic origin, to finish with the agricultural landscape.

The structure is determined by two mountain massifs to the north and to the south. They are connected by a land gangway or way through low and undulate lands. Notorious are the alignment of volcanic cones which are hardly touch by the erosion. This gangway is covered in greater part by sands which penetrates through *Penedo* Bay and by blowing away, it cut across the island until hitting the shore at the opposite bank. This is called *Jable* (Chimbs).

In the North, the *Famara* Massif prevails with 20 kilometres lons from north to south and 4 kilometres wide. *Castillejo* pick has a reaching submit of 668 m. at the *Chache* cliff. A few prehistoric volcanoes are located on this massif, being *La Corona* and the huge lava field (taking some sq kilometres over the sea) are the most outstanding and most eye-catching in this area.

In the South, the *Femés* massif is the one which marks the most elevate orography. It has 10 kilometres long from north to south and 5 kilometres wide, ending at *Hacha Grande* with 561 m. The rest is a plain ending in a coast spreading with beaches.

Volcanic risk. It can be defined as the result of multiplying the probability of a certain volcanic phenomenon that can happen by the resulting damages.

At present, it is difficult to determine accurately the probability of eruption of a volcano. We will summarize the danger related to each of the eruption types that can take place:

The emission of lava causes economic damages but it is the less dangerous phenomenon for human lives. The displacement speed of lava has always been quite low. It depends on the emission speed of the eruptive mouth, the slope, and the viscosity of the lava.

The emission of pyroclastic products can adopt very different modalities. In general pumice stone and ashy are thrown. In spite of that it is not the most dangerous phase. A collapse can be cause by an excessive accumulation of ashes on the roofs of buildings. Although it is possible to remain under the ashy and pumice stone rain. The worst would be to be caught in closed places with no air.

Other more dangerous phenomenons happen during the explosive phases. If the pressure of the gases, which the volcanic column forms, it diminishes suddenly, the materials containing the column fall. The mixture of solid and gassy products have great mobility and they can slip swiftly. This phenomenon is denominated pyroclastic flow. Another phenomenon is the so-called impact wave. It is a ring of gas in quick expansion surrounding the base of the volcanic column. It is, generally, the interaction of the magma and the water. It is characterized by the quick expansion dragging along ashy and solid materials. The initial speed can reach 180 Km/h., what explains the great destructive capacity.

The caldera of mud, is due to the crumbling of pyroclastic material accumulated in the volcanic column and soaked in water. The water can come directly from the issued vapors or from later rains. The destructiveness is due so much to the great mobility as to the high specific weight.

Many eruptions come preceded by a series of premonitory called phenomenons manifesting in weeks, even months, before the eruption starts. The ascension of the magma comes accompanied by earthquakes of low and medium intensity. The volcano begins to be deformed and often there is an increase of activity of the fumarole and the temperature. However this doesn't mean that an eruption will take place, but rather the eruption probability has increased.

Volcanic area of Timanfaya. Cones alignment from Montaña Rajada to Montaña del Fuego.

Lanzarote is known as the island of a hundred volcanoes (exactly 110 volcanoes are registered). Most of them are located in the centre area, delimited on the north by the line that goes from *Penedo* bay, going through *Guanapay* mountain, to finish at *Guatiza* mountain. And on the south, from *Avila* bay to *Janubio* lake going through Yaiza. The most characteristic center spots of this area are: From north to south the small alignment of cones in the region of Soo, with *Caldera Trasera* (293 m.) as a dominant point. Going further to the east, the old *Caldera del Cuchillo*, a round cone with small wall height and with more than 1 km. wide. Its flat floor is made of farming land and its the most elevated point reaches 181 m. There are a series of volcanic cones unequally distributed or forming short alignments. *Tenezar* mountain (368 m.) is one of the most important. Its hillside expands to the coast where the marine erosion had carved out a extensive creek. Near Tinguatón village appears another cone alignment: *Quemada* Mountain, *Caldera Quemada*, *El Filete*, *Coruja* Mountain and *Rostros* Mountain. Between Tiagua and Tao are: *Clérigo* Mountain and *Perneo* Peak, belonging to the 1824 eruptions and where a beautiful panoramic is observed. On the west *Tamia* Mountain is found surrounding Tao. It is a half-round caldera with 500 m. high. The big volcano alignment with more than 47 km. length, distant from the surroundings of Guatiza to the *Pechiguera* point. The volcanoes from this alignment don't constitute a

straight chain nor continued, neither the same age. Its disposition isn't casual yet is the result to the existence of a volcanic fault. Another shot alignment with about 4 km. length is the so-called *Zonzamas* group. It is the main one from the mountain group with 329 m. high. To the west *Montaña Blanca* (556 m.) with a cone shape. It is very notorious since is one of the highest mountain of Lanzarote. Finally, all the areas from *Parque Nacional de Timanfaya* (Timanfaya National Park) has almost 30 recent volcanic cones lined up in various crack formations. This area will be described later on.

As it was mentioned previously, the Canarian Volcanism Periods present no specific rhythm, yet any day and in somewhere the ground can be broken by the gas pressures and start releasing lava. These eruptions last few days as it is proved in the later five hundred years of history. As a sole exemption, the *Timanfaya* eruption last six years in Lanzarote.

Regarding the seashore, between *Punta* (point) *Fariones* and Arrecife, in general, the island eastern coast is a rocky low coast. It is formed by a demolishing *malpaís* (lava field) and it is very stricken by the wind, except in *Punta Fariones* surrounding and the *Ancones* cliff with 50 m high. The meridional coast, between Arrecife and *Playa Quemada* it has the same characteristics of low coast, with extensive beach formations. At the south eastern extreme, the cliffs between *Playa Quemada* and *Punta del Papagayo* are more or less high, interrupted by some beaches in the south area. The south coast is fairly smoothen until *Punta Pechiguera* with noteworthy beaches like *Las Mujeres, Papagayo*, and *Las Coloradas*. The same type of low cliff coasts but without beaches, continue to the eastern and north- eastern of the island until *Punta Penedo*, interrupted only by the *Janubio* and *Golfo* lagoons. A section of low coast, with a very important beach called *Famara*, it is extended between *Punta Penedo* and *Punta Ganada*. High cliffs, up to 500 m. in some areas, appears from *Famara* beach until *Punta de Fariones*. These cliffs are getting smoothen until constituting a low coast in the *Risco* beach area and *Río* salt flats, with a sedimentary formation in front of La Graciosa island.

The practice of agriculture is subject to the shortage of rain (144 mm. yearly), and to the irregular distribution of rain throughout the year. Also it is conditioned by the wind, and the shortage of developed land. This exceptionally hostile environment has encouraged the invention of the island inhabitant (called in a familiar way *majoreros* o *conejeros*) up to the point of forcing to develop farming techniques and to create agricultural landscape in perfect rhythm with the medium.

The recognised agricultural landscape types in the island are as follow:

- Vineyard and fig farming dug in the recent lava and surround by artificial walls of volcanic stone. They characterise areas like *La Geria* in the center of the island. With no doubt these are the most outstanding of the island, not only for the landscapes yet for the techniques.

- Artificial lapillus sandy bank agriculture, generally with onions, bordered by square volcanic stones take up by grapevine.

- Farming in the *Jable* (Chimbs), covering of large areas by organic sand formations created by winds), mainly with sweet potatoes and watermelon. The lining of bushes are protected from the wind by stalk line up, planting out cereal or small reeds.

- Prickly pear or nopal farming on artificial sand-bank prepared for the growing and afterwards the recollection of the *cochinilla* (cochineal) . Normally they are enclosed by volcanic stone walls and they are located usually in Mala and Guatiza areas.

- Farming in the sedimentary plains. They are showier than the previous ones but contain the best land. The best example is the Haría valley, which even surprises because of its great palm trees.

- Lastly, the farming in tableland on the hillside. It is uncommonly profitable and the high effort of keeping it force the farmers to abandon which cause a fast damage of the landscaping. They are commonly located in the ravines in the north area.

Although the entire island presents a high natural landscaping value, the previous factors have determined a variety of areas in which the landscape has more "quality" since represents these mentioned

Bay of Penedo. artificial sand-bank, cliffs of Famara, La Graciosa, and Montaña Clara.

Crop of vineyards in La Geria.

factors. In order to select the foresaid areas we have taken in consideration the following: what and the quality what is been seeing, and the degree of visual change. These areas are: *La Corona* Volcano and its surrounding; *malpaís* (lava field) and subsequent fields of farming. Mountainous Massif of *La Quemada*, until the point of *La Cantería, Riscos de Famara*. Valleys of *Guinate, Temisa* and *Barranco Hondo*. Valley and palm trees of Haría and its surrounding: *La Atalaya* and Mountain of *Llanos, Bermeja* Mountain, *Roja* Mountain, *Tamia, Timbaiba, Tersa, Blanca* and *Guatiza, Mina, Zonzamas* and *Maneje. La Geria* in the area of Tías. *Masdache* Volcano and its surroundings. *Punta del Papagayo, Los Ajaches* Massif, Ravine of *Tenegüime*, Volcano and *Malpaís of Timanfaya*, La Graciosa, and the islets.

　　Likewise there are singular elements with great and accurate power to be mentioned here: for the reduced space quality, for the harmony or because of cultural and didactic interest, as well as the sightseeing from where it can be seen an expanding panoramic (all of them with an easy access): *Salinas* (salt-flats) *del Janubio, Los Hervideros, El Golfo*, National Park of *Timanfaya*, The agricultural village of *El Patio, Famara* Beach, *Guinate* watch-tower, *Salinas del Río, Las Conchas* Beaches (La Graciosa), *Haría* watch-tower (km. 23 from Arrecife-Haría road). *Río* watch-tower. *La Corona* Volcano. *Cueva de los Verdes. Jameos del Agua*. Garden of Cactus. Casttle of San Gabriel. Casttle of San José and *Femés* watch-tower.

Contrast with Las Conchas beach.

NATURAL RESOURCES

Climate. Sub-dessert climate, characterized by the lack of raining (140 mm. annually) and by the frequency of the trade winds. This arrangement must be differentiating. Since the ocean and the thermic-regulator effects (as a consequence of the cold Canary current) make the climate considerably smooth. And being the average annual temperature between 20° to 16° C, with minimum thermic deflection. January is the coldest month while August is the hottest month of the year.

Because of the sub-tropical location, Canary Islands are affected almost all year around, specially during summer time, by the anticyclones (high pressure air). The one that affects to the islands are called Azones anticyclone which is responsible for the Trade Winds (N-E). The Trade Winds are overload with humidity and salt, with frequent cloudiness of horizontal development due to it's long track through the ocean. The Trade Winds increase the speed because of the obstacles of the island structure. The average speed of the Trade Winds is 23 km/h. Formerly, the Trade Winds were suitable to elevate the ocean water to the terraces of salt flats as well as to mill the grain with the ones to make *gofio* (typical local food).

The Trade Winds have to different stratums: inferior trade wind which is characterized as humid and cool and it has a density between 1.200 to 1.800 m. high.

The superior trade wind (N-W) is characterized as warm and dry. Since Lanzarote doesn't go over the mentioned high, therefore it is not touched upon this last stratum and the humidity is practically constant all over the island. The temperature difference between these two stratums provokes the cumulated-stratum formation.

When the Trade Wind disappears, the winds change direction and origin, having different start points: Atlantic origin (S-E) or polar (N or N-E), which provokes the minimum temperatures of the year. The Trade Wind is called *"gota fría"* (cold air pockets) when has a polar origin. Moreover the majority of the rain: tropical continental origin, from Africa, it is what is so-called *"tiempo sur or levante"* (South weather or east wind) and generally comes with dust in the air.

The high degree of insulation is another outstanding element of the climate presenting an annual average of 250 h. Relative humidity swings around 70%, lessen the strong dryness. The rains, as were mentioned previously, are short and happen from September to May. The most raining month is January and the less raining month is August. The storm are not frequent at all.

The water temperature fluctuates between 17° to 23° C on the surface. Ocean currents are more intense and persistent on the leeward side and flow most of the time from NE to SW direction, parallel to the shores of the island.

Habitat and Island Evolution.

The Canary Island are included in the biogeo-graphical area known as Macaronesia, a term derived from the Greek (Makaros =happy, and nesos=island). This grouping is made up of five Atlantic archipelagos (Madeira, Azores, Salvajes, Canary Islands and Cabo Verde). The area, taken as a whole, is marked by an significant affinity of the flora and fauna.

The majority of the archipelago's plants and animals come from African and European origins. While the flora and fauna of these continents were adapted to profound climatic changes over the past few thousands years. The Atlantic archipelagos of Macaronesia maintained a great diversity of habitats and a relative climatic stability. These conditions allowed the survival of species disappearing from the surrounding areas, and in some cases, from the rest of the world. At the same time, new species evolved having origin from the ones that had arrived earlier.

The Canary Islands became a living museum, with species and ecosystems of an earlier area, exhibiting abundant examples of evolution in the islands and the creative capacity of nature. Had it not been for the famous quarantine that prevented Darwing from reaching the islands, this author would have found sufficient arguments for the mechanisms of evolution in anticipation of the discoveries he would later make

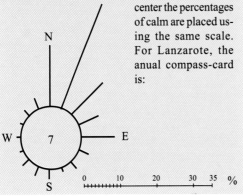

Relative humidity is the percentual quotient among the quantities of water vapor from the air to a certain temperature. And the maximum quantity of water vapor the air could contain to that temperature.

The **compass-card** consists on placing the corresponding frequency -expressed in % - for each direction of the wind to every month, obtaining the monthly average. Or for every year, being the result of the annual average compass-card. In the center the percentages of calm are placed using the same scale. For Lanzarote, the anual compass-card is:

Clouds on Chinijo Archipelago.

in South America and the Galapagos Islands. If this is not enough, the abundance of vertebrate fauna in the Canary islands, among reptiles and birds, one finds similar examples to those used to demonstrate the famous Theory of Evolution. In contrast of this relative poverty, it is remarkable the tremendous botany treasure and the invertebrate fauna, so that even today new species are being discovered and added to the Canary's and the world's natural patrimony.

This tremendous interest generated by the nature in the Canary Islands has been documented historically through the visits and works of prestigious researchers (HUMBOLDT, WEBB, VIERA AND CLAVIJO…), just as many of the islands' habitat testimony been declared Human Heritage Sites (El Cedro) and World Biosphere Reserves (Los Tilos Forest and the island of Lanzarote).

On October 7th, 1993, this island was declared Biosphere Reserve by the UNESCO. This implies a recognition of its singular values and natural characteristics, and to value the island inhabitant role as warrant of the island preservation.

The purpose of reaching a "permanent" and equitable development has and continue been one of the more complex and urgent enterprise to be confronted by the human being reaching the XXI century. It is well understood the term "permanent development" as the one capable to satisfy the needs of the present generation, without comprises the capacity of the future generation to satisfy the present needs.

From 1976 the first Biosphere Reserves were declared. Since then 305 territories from 78 countries were declared Biosphere Reserves.

Flora. About 612 species of Vascular plants are well-known (braken and flowered plants). These plants grow in a spontaneous manner in this island. The majority of these plants belong to aboriginal. Among those 93 are endemic, out of 20 are considered exclusive from Lanzarote and 24 are shared with Fuerteventura.

In spite of Lanzarote endemic flora is not enough comparing with the entirety of the canary archipelago, where there are 650 endemic species in about 7,200 sq kilometres, the result is very rich and varied when comparing with any European country. About 100 endemic species exist in France with 560,000 sq kilometres extension. About 16 endemic species exist in Great Britain with 250,000 sq kilometres extension. And only 6 exist in Germany with 350,000 sq km. extension. With all of these data, the flora importance of the island is well clear.

The islands' vegetation is structured according to a pattern of "floors" conditioned by the constant flow of humid trade winds and the elevations of the land masses. Lanzarote barely exceed 600 m. above sea level at the summit of the oldest mountains. With the result that the winds usually pass over without releasing the moisture. In contrast to the forest found on the more altitudinous islands of the archipelago, Lanzarote offers

17

Anchored Balancones (Traganum Moquinii) in dunes. Behind the beach of Famara.

best examples of the sub-desert habitats of the so-called "Canary Basal Floor". Lanzarote flora patrimony is very poor, not only for the aridity of its climate but also for the devastation of the human action and the excessive pasturing. Moreover the natural settlement, for lack of time, stays (as the beginning of its ecological evolution) in a great area covered by recent materials from the historical and pre-historical eruptions.

Nowadays, the slow improvement of the deeply transformed vegetable community is being possible due to the decline of agriculture and pasturing, as well as a greatest human awakening that has concluded to the protection of broadening areas. Today we see a dynamic landscape evolving towards its original form, whose vestiges were preserved in inaccessible and or scarcely productive areas.

The most interesting areas are located in the cliff of *Famara, Los Ajaches, Malpaís of La Corona,* organic sand beaches (North beaches, white sand beaches, areas of *Papagayo*, etc.), and the vegetal settlement process and floor formation that are taking places in the area of *Timanfaya*.

The Thorny brush is a plant form most widely found on the island, growing on the plains and low hills, as well as inundisturbed areas such as previously cultivated fields, commonly called "*malezas*" (undergrowth). In the re-colonization of these spaces, the hardiness of the furze (Launaea Arborescens) has made it one of the foremost elements of brush in the ecological order. For this reason it has become one of the most common species of the island, almost to the

point of dominating certain areas of brush. In the better conserved areas there is a greater diversity, including plant forms such as hawthorn (Lycium Intrincatum), Matamoros (Suaeda Vera), and rama or brusca (Rhamnus Crenulata), among others.

Verodes (Senecio Kleinia), *tabaibas* (Euphorbia Balsamifera) and *bejeques* (Aeonium nobile) represent the purest vestigial plant forms, and are believed to be indigenous. The tabaibal generally grows on the slopes and foot of hills and escarpments, though more recent varieties have taken to the recently lava fields and the islets. Among these, the sweet tabaiba prefers areas affected by ocean breezes.

The palms is practically the only example of indigenous tree forms, usually found in ravines, valleys and especially, along the old cultivated terraces "*gavias*". The great Palm Trees of Haría has a special attention, located in the surroundings of the town and near farms. Out of approximately 10,000 palms in the past, only 5,000 examples are left at present.

Canary basal floor. Semi-arid mediterranean climate vegetation with rains among 100-300 mm. 20 º C average temperature. High insolation. With loamy, saline or calcareous floors (*caliches*). Example: arid pastures, *heaths xerófilos* (storing water plant), euphorbias canariences, euphorbias sp., arthrpchemum fruticosum.

Uva de mar in coast of black sand.

In areas of marshland and salt marshes, periodically flood by the tides one finds another natural habitat of special interest with a special vegetation formed with plants very reach with species like *salado* (Schicozogyne Glaberrima), *saladillo* (Jubera Canariensis), *mato* (Lavandula Canariensis) and *tebete* (Beta Patellaris) among others; the importance of the salt marsh lies precisely in its character as a wetland, and in turn, its connection with birds.

The sandy environments has as well a wide vegetal representation and it can be divided in two different areas: the coasts and the dune fields extended towards the interior.

The coasts and dunes can also be divided, according to their colour and the geological nature of their components, into two kinds: black sands and clear sands. The latest have a floral richness that is scarcely or not present in the previous ones. The white sand coast has its own floral community, among are: the *Uva de Mar* (Zygophyllum Fontanesii) with fleshy Y shaped leaves, Sea lettuce, *Cebollin de playa* (Androcymbium Psammophilum), some *euforbias* (spurges), Sea sprouts and the *balancones* (Traganum Maquinii), which help the dune formation with great sizes and volume (2 to 3 meter high and 4 or 5 meter diameter thickness). This specie is found on established dunes beyond the beach of *Famara*.

The dune fields extend towards the interior in accordance with the prevailing winds (the *jable*), the tremendous aridity and friction caused by the movement of sand, and the high grade of isolation and the salinity which greatly limit the settlement for living beings. Nevertheless the *corazoncillos* (Lotus Lanzarotensis), Ononix, *algahuera* (Bassia tormentosa), *criadilla* (Terferzia Pinoyi), *melosas* (Ononix Natrix), etc. can survive.

The vegetation of the coast cliffs are compounded by adapted species to live almost all over the year in a hard condition. These communities are limited by the wind, the salty humidity, the floor shortage, and the geological instability with a specific number of species. The most representative areas of this kind of environment are the cliff of Famara. Referring to the density of the vegetal layer, its flora is not exuberant but the number of species predictably overpass. Some bracken and numerous moss, and lichens can be added to a list of approximately 230 species of plants with flowers. Within this unit can be distinguished some areas:

1. Cost Platform. With specific species from the clear color sandy coastal environment.

2. Slope (*piedemonte*). Occupied by a dispersed *tabaibal* and *salado matogota* (Arthrochemum Fruticosum) fundamentally, in a lower areas. Above 150 m. it changes to species as verodes (Kleinia Neriifolia), *cornical* (Periploca laevigata), *heliantemos* (helianthemus), thorns, gorses, *corazoncillos* (Lotus Lanzarotensi), spear, everlasting flowers, bugle, etc..

3. Cliffs above 300 m. With everlasting flowers, *bejeques*, *garbancillos* (a kind of shrub), shrub kind, sow-thistle, swine-thistle, etc...

4. Deep ravines. With bitter *tabaibas* and *senecios* among others.

Therefore and as it can be proven it has a great botanical interest.

bejeque (Aeonium nobile) in bloom.

Lichens.

Abandoned farming colonized by verodes (Kleinia Neriifolia). North of the island.

The cliffs of Guinate-Famara, long time ago, had heath, and bay leaf, that is to say vestiges of an arboraceous formation which survives very few samples.

The lava fields configure another botanical atmosphere of great importance. The colonization process has already begun, still hardly perceptible in most of the surface. Although this process will determine the existence of an alive covering in hundred or thousands of years according to the environment possibilities. We will divide two areas according to the antiquity of the lava: prehistoric lava very colonized, as the *Malpaís* of *La Corona*; and historical lava at the beginning of the vegetable process, as the *Timanfaya*.

The most typical vegetable formations are the tabaibales in the *Malpaís* of *La Corona*. According to the height it changes from being sweet to bitter:

1. The sweet *tabaiba* prevails below 100 m. and the rest of the vegetable composition is relatively low, with some *verodes* samples, gorses, thorns and saltwort.

Similar to this type there are other *tabaibales* in the west of the island.

2. The bitter *tabaiba* dominates above the 100 m. among some *verodes*, common sorrel, gorses, helianthemun, etc.. Vegetation that reaches the volcano summit.

The vegetable colonization takes place from two different sources in *Timanfaya*: the natural development by means of the conquest of the mineral world and for the expansion of the surviving plants which were not affected by the eruptions.

The lichens begin the first phase of the plant succession and they transform the ground. Therefor, allowing and facilitating the superior plants settlement with demands of a more developed substrate. Of these superior plants there is no much to point out. Only the tabaibales deserve to be outstanding and some samples of sea grape that are developed in the coast. On the other hand, 71 species different from lichens are classified.

Furthermore the lichens are the main characters of the wide rocky fields stretching over the plains, hillocks and slopes in the rocky escarpments, and of course, in one of the environments most identified with the islands, the *malpaises* (lava fields). Two lichens with a somewhat more complex structure are the *aicán* (Roccella) and the archill formerly exploded as a source of dye. They colonize the inaccessible parts of cliffs oriented to the north.

The more important plant manifestations in the National Park of Timanfaya are in the islets. They represent a true "oasis" compared with the surroundings. Within the P.N. 239 different species are listed: 8 are endemic from Lanzarote, 7 from Lanzarote and Fuerteventura, 13 from Canary, and 6 macaronesics.

Therefore, the Lanzarote vegetable wealth although verifiable in data, it is characterized by the scarce perceptibility in the landscape. Some "treasures" are hided in the highest parts in Famara, amid inhospitable lava or in arid sands.

Fortunately, the Canary environmental normative provides at the present time the regulations and the protection of spaces and species of the Natural Patrimony, setting out the consequences of possible violations. In spite of this, individual responsibility stemming from personal commitment plays a far more important role in search of the Patrimony conservation.

Fauna. Without doubt, the **invertebrates** and among them the insects , are the faunistic group best represented in the canary archipelago and therefore in this island.

In the Canary Islands, more than 5.000 species of this group have been cited, some 10% endemic, which, in the case of beetles rises as high as 35% . As far as beetles, fly, cricket, spires, grasshopper, etc. variety concern, are be present at any spot one can pay attention to find these small animals. Even in the inhospitable recent lava of the Timanfaya they are counted 120 different species. Among the insects, two species are particularly noteworthy, one a fossil, the *antophoras* bee, the other living, the *cochinillas* (Cochineal insect), both having special relevance to the landscape.

The Antophoras Bee were insects similar to present day wasps, that made cavities in the sand where larval development then took place. The fossilized remains of these "nests" are today found in great quantities in the interior, recognizable as small clumps of compressed sand, hollow and ellipsoidal.

The small white spots that appear on the leaves of the prickly pear-cactus are the female of the cochineal, an insect of great economic importance in the past, due to the highly valued carmín dye it produced. This insect became protected by law in 1827. The present importance of such products is being re-evaluated due to studies which have shown the health risks involved in the use of much cheaper artificial substance.

In spite the numerous invertebrates, the Canary Islands are not blessed with an abundance of **vertebrates**, birds being the only group represented by a great number of species. In the context of the archipelago, Lanzarote and its islets have the best representative birds, with an important number of nesting (many endemic) and migratory species. The strategic location of the islands, as an area of passage and winter stopover at the extreme end of a migratory route, lends to their wetland areas a more than local

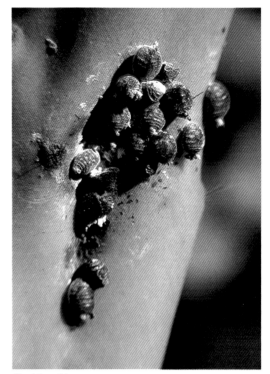

Cochineal insects.

significance. Its coasts, salt marshes, ponds and lagoons are " lodging area" for numerous species, a community whose membership changes with the seasons.

The different habitats receiving the variety of birds are as follow:

1. The islets. These are become the reserve zone to host any threaten specie from the biggest islands. The more outstanding nesting species and more interesting to preserve are: cory's shearwater, argentum gull, storm petrel, Bulwer' petrel, many shearwater, Madeiras petrel, stonechat, titlark in *malpaises* and close to the beaches, lesser short-toed lark in earthy and sandy plain areas, Eleonor falcon, and *osprey* commonly named *guincho*. The greater habitats of *guincho* from all the archipelago are located in these islets.

2. Sandy and rocky plains. Among others, goldfinch, greenfinch, linnets, fallow finch, blue tit, grey shrike, abudillas or hoopoe, stone curlew, cream-coloured courser and houbara bustard or great bustard are found in this open spaces, where farming and bushes are profuse.

3. Mountains. The most significant species are: osprey, egyptian vulture, Eleonor and Berbería falcon, buzzard, kestrel, as well as raven. The latest can be seen in any area due to the abundance of this specie, but they are more present close to the mountains and hillside of ravines where they nest.

Guirre (Egyptian Vulture).

Bisbitas (Titlark).

4. Salt marshes, marshes and coast areas. The birds most noteworthy of these areas are: shearwater and turnstone plover, grey plover, dunlin and little egret as migratory birds. The special mention are the few common terns left from the numerous existent community earlier.

5. Malpaises. The topographic resources shortage makes this area a poor location for nesting. Nevertheless, 20 nesting species are located: egyptian vulture, kestrel, barbary partridge, rock dove, turtle dove, barn owl, hoopoe, road bird, sedge warbler, trumpeter bullfinch, ….

6. Ravines. Best protected areas for small birds like spanish sparrow which they are located as well in populated habitat, *vencejo pálido y unicolor* (family Apodidae of swift), barn owl, buzzard and kestrel.

Reptiles are present in the form of lizards, the *"lisnejas"* or *"lisa majorera"* (thought to be endemic to Lanzarote and Fuerteventura), and *"perenquenes"* or geckos, seen on walls and close to bright lights.

The amphibians are represented by the common frog, which requires moist areas of fresh water (ponds, ditches, etc.) in order to survive.

With respect to the mammals that inhabit the island, all were introduced, voluntary or involuntarily by men, with the exception of the bats, who managed to get there on their own. In this mammals section includes the domestic animals like dog, cat, goat, sheep, horse, dromedary and donkey.

Undomesticated animals are found throughout the island, including hedgehogs, shrews, bat, rabbit, mouse and rat.

The special attention given to the **marine fauna** for so long is due to a very practical consideration: fishing. More recently, however, it has developed a greater scientific and technical interest of the marine environments, fact that has carried on to protect legally certain coast areas of Lanzarote and its islets.

Some 390 species divided into 117 families have been classified in the island. Naturally, it is not possible to mention all of them here, but we can at least give a few facts. First with respect to the ecosystems and waters surrounding the island. Then with regards to the most representative species living in them.

Due to the Canary geographical location, close to the African coasts, and the fact that it is located in the way through of the *Golfo* current (Canary cold current), the local waters present anomalies of salinity and temperature which greatly influence marine life. These waters permit the existence of species, vegetable as animals, from different regions. It is possible to identify two distinct ecosystems, the *Barlovento* (windward) sea or the north which, conventionally, is situated between *Pechiguera* Point and *Fariones* Point; and the south or *Sotavento* (leeward) sea, between *Fariones* Point and *Papagayo* Point. Between *Papagayo* Point and *Pechiguera* Point there is a completely open stretch of water that can be considered an area of transition.

The differences between the two zones do not lie solely in the nature of the bottoms, sandy as opposed to rocky, (what the fishermen from the island refer to as *"marisco"*), or in the surge and swell that affect the windward coast for most of the year, but also rather in the quality of the water. On the north side is slightly cooler and much richer in plankton. This results in a greater abundance and diversity of marine life as well as a variety of species. Adding more, the North sea is less fished. Some species are characteristic of the north sea.

The majority of the species are "creoles", bound to the island for their entire life cycle. The rest, fishes

22

that "travel", as the seamen say, are frequent visitors: tuna fishes, dolphin-fishes, sardines, snipe fishes and various species of sharks, all of which at certain times of the year are found in these waters.

By families, the sea breams predominate: bogues, salemas, white sea breams, black sea breams, saddled breams, red banded sea breams, pink dentex, common pandoras, common sea breams, axillary sea breams, etc. These species are typical of the platform.

The second family -family being used here in a vernacular meaning- by number of species is that of the sharks. The majority are "creole" and live on the bottom, as is the case with smoodith-hounds, spurdogs, gulper sharks, kitefin sharks, blackmouth catsharks, etc. Referring to the "travellers" sharks, the most abundant are scalloped hammerheads, shortfin makos and blue sharks.

In the "*mariscos*", well represented are the groupers, not so much for their variety as their abundance: dusky groupers, combers, comb groupers, etc. And the wrasses: ornate wrasses, rainbow wrasses, scale-rayed wrasses, etc.

The tuna fishes and the like are represented mainly by skipjack tunas, atlantic bluefin tunas, yellowfin tunas and atlantic bonitos, in addition to yellowmouth barracudas and the highly abundant chub mackerels.

Among other species not included in the above mentioned families, the most important are:

On the platform: lesser weevers, african striped grunts, alfonsinos, grey triggerfishes, thinlip grey mullets, fangtooth morays, striped red mullets, fusca drums and parrot-fishes, among others.

On the *veril* (verge) and their proximity: conger eels, stone basses, silver scabbardfishes, mora moros and alfonsinos of deep water, being the most representative.

The pelagic: halfbreaks, flying fishes, dolphin fishes, blue fishes, swordfishes, sardines and snipe fishes.

Moray surrounding by Alfonsino fishes.

The crustaceans are represented by a multitude of species. The best known are:

Among the crabs: the sider crabs, which are frequently caught in traps lowered to shallow depths: the white and red crabs, widely sought for their exquisite meat, caught by hand from the shore on moonless nights at low tide: The xantho porssa, found under rocks on the shore and used as bait to catch parrot fishes and red banded sea breams.

Shrimps are noteworthy for their great abundance.

Often found in the north sea caves are the Canary lobsters, known locally as "*bogavantes*". In the shady areas of the north sea surfes, barnacles are found in abundance. The older folks call them "*patas de cabra*" (goats feet).

Regarding to shellfish, mussels are more abundant and the leeward coast of the island is covered with them. Around the entire perimeter of Lanzarote, snails, kind of snails, and limpets are also plentifully found.

Beneath rocks near the shore there are "*orejas de mar*" (sea ears), very colourful, which people from the island, "*majorejos*", refer to as "*almejas*", clams (one valve). Endless varieties of snails and other cones are also to be found.

Among the cephalopodos, specially octopus, squid and cuttlefishes are abundant.

Far from the shore, sea turtles are often seen, especially the careta turtles, and occasionally the laud turtle, which nest o some beaches.

The most common marine mammals are the "*toninas*" or dolphins, some whales, and recently the occasionally presence of seals.

Better emphasising the marine invertebrates living in the marine lagoons of "*jameos*" of *Agua* and the *Lagos*. The latest researches about this section indicate that more than 30 species, out of half are still unknown for scientific. Among them are the famous blind crab or "*jameito*", which became the Lanzarote animal symbol.

Fishing. The idea of writing on this topic arises not only for the economic importance, but as well, from the necessity to limit man's depreciating influence on the natural fishery and marine life resources of the island. It is hoped that all can enjoy, and at the same time respect the maritime richness of Lanzarote, for the good of the island and, ultimately, for the good of its inhabitants. For that reason, a translation of the Shellfish and Fishing Regulation of the Autonomous Community is offered.

Canary Island Mussels Shell Fishing. The minimum size permitted for capture is 7 cm. Measured

Fishing boats in Puerto Naos (Pier Naos).

on the longest dimension. In addition, there are annual periods of closed season from April 1st. to June 30th and from September 1st to November 30th during which the capture of mussels is absolutely prohibited.

The maximum catch per person per day is 10 kg. And the cutting tool may not have a width greater than 7 cm.

Coastal Professional Fishing. Any fishing method involving dragging, as well as any dragging technique practising with vessels or from the shore are prohibited. The use of nets, especially the so-called "*trasmallo*" (trammel net) are prohibit.

Fishing with traps are permitted but this technique is in the way to be extinguished. 25 is the allowed number, which nets must have size of 2m diameter . Every boat owner must make a declaration to the Fishing Association of the number of used traps, size and the depth at which they will be used. Nets must be identified with plates which show the embarkation identification number and ship owner identification mark. The minimum mesh opening is 31.6 mm. and minimum depth allowed is 18 m.

Completely prohibit in any area determined by the Fishing Local Council, furthermore in *Bocaina,* from *Pechiguera* Point to *Papagayo* Point, and in *Chinijo* Archipelago.

For "shrimp traps" different criteria are used. The mesh opening will have a minimum of 10 mm.

per side, with shrimp mouth and maximum of three traps per crew member in each embarkation.

Fish-trap as called "*tambor*" (drum), for fangtooth moray to be captured. Prohibited in less than 5m. depth and the number is limited by the Fishing Local Board.

The so-called "*Palangre*" (Multi-hook line fishing) is permitted, but not more than 500 hooks per boat may be used simultaneously. The closure of coves, bays, etc. or any activity which has its amim the corralling of fishes in a specific place.

Details on the minimum size permitted for each species are available in every port from the Local Fishing Council or the Fishermen's Association.

Recreational Fishing area in the coastal area:

Submarine fishing. It is prohibit at night, the use of scuba equipment, propulsion devises, electric or explosive tips: Neither the use of any type of tackle. Catch is limited to 5 kg. per person per day or 25 kg. for groups of five or more.

At the same time it is prohibit this activity not less than 250 m. of distance among people including the fishermen on the surface.

Submarine fishing is permitted all year around in the following areas:

- From *Pasito* Point to *Ancones* Point (*Tierra Negra* Point).

- From *Tiñosa* Point to *Papagayo* Point.
- From *Jurado* Point to *Gaviota* Point.

Rod Fishing. Not more than three hooks per device, lashing, rope or similar device or two rods per person are allowed at one time. Girding fishing, net fishing, dragging, "*palangres*" (long line), nets, tramps, "*güelderas*" and any other similar are permitted.

Catch is limited to 4 kg. per person per day, or one large fish. Groups of more than four persons are limited to 16 kg. per day.

Deep Sea Fishing. Prohibited within half a mile of professional fishing vessels. Catch is limited to three fishes per person and per day (weight is not limited).

In any of the three cases previously mentioned, the captures are limited to personal consumption, and sale of catch is prohibited. Sport fishermen may not transport more than 10 kg. of fish between islands. Recreational fishermen are required to obtain a license from the Fishing Office.

The island's fishermen are organized into three fraternities (*in spanish called Cofradías*):
- *Cofradía* San Ginés in Arrecife. Address: Puerto Naos Avenue. Fisherman Wharf. Arrieta, Punta Mujeres, Orzola, La Caleta de Famara, La Santa and Puerto del Carmen and Charco anchor of San Ginés and Juan Rejón in Arrecife are the circuits of this *Cofradía*.

- *Cofradía* La Graciosa. Caleta del Sebo, La Graciosa.
- *Cofradía* Playa Blanca. Playa Blanca.Yaiza.

In Lanzarote the so-called "artesian fishing" is practically the only method of commercial fishing. The fleet is composed of *barquillos* or *falúas*, small boats up to two tons, generally powered by a 25 hp. Diesel engine. There are usually two crew members per boat. The work time generally does not exceed 24 hours, and at the end of it, the boats are left on the beach or at anchor, depending on the weather. They are not equipped with navigation devices or mechanized systems for fishing: all the work is done by manpower alone, though some have crude devices which assist hauling in the fish traps.

From the first half of the present century a fishing float was developed in Arrecife working in a Canarian-Saharian bank. This float that still continues, and the industry of "*salpreso*" (salty fish), already disappeared, contributed to the capital city development. The canned goods and preserve factories attracted the people from the country, and the result was the most important economic development in Lanzarote prior to tourism.

The salty fish "*en rama*" (in a stick) preparation was carried out on board with archaic method of definitive preservation. This preparation was consisted on washing, salting, and piling up.

Dock of La Santa.

The following is a summary of some of the techniques and types of fishing, beginning with the simplest one:

- The oldest technique of all is of scattering the sap in the puddle of the *tabaiba dulce* (sweet euphorbia) crushing to expel the milk The fishes like white sea bream, scale-rayed wrasses, etc. get "drunk" with this milk. The left over fish was not sold but was prepared with salt to be sold later.

- *Apañada de Toninas*.- Type of fishing in "corrals". The fishermen thrashed and stoned the dolphin banks called toninas to force them to enter in the Arrecife peer. Once they are corralled the fishermen harpooned them in a non-deep water.

At present, these two fishing techniques are not in use anymore.

- *Fija*.- An iron or steel rod with one or several end points, used for catching octopus in the pools left by the tide when it withdraws.

- *Gueldera* or *Tarralla*.- A large sack of fabric or metallic mesh supported by a metal hoop. It is hung from a thick flexible pole using four strands of fishing lines. It is used for catching the *carnada* (bait): bogues, chub mackerels and blue jack mackerels. Such fishing is done from the boat.

- *Nasas*.- A trap of iron framework and metallic fabric. Those used in the island are round and vary in size according to their use. They have two openings or "*nasillos*", and a door for removing the fish. It is the device most commonly employed in these waters, and in fact, the most deadly. Nasas are effective at any depth and on any type of bottom.

- *Chinchorro*.- A type of trawling net comprised of two bands and a pouch that is manipulated from the shore or from a boat anchored close to the shore. It is used for catching small fishes of different species: bogues, chubs, sardines, striped red mullets, axillary sea breams, etc.

- *Albacora* (Little Tunny) Fishing.- It is done during the daytime, far from the coast, usually near the sea banks. The boats anchor or drift, depending on the tides and the location of fishes. It is used the *liñas* (a line with a shiny hook) of varying thickness provided in the last two or three fathoms of a strong *arganero* (steel cable), with straight, strong hooks. Usually two or three of these liñas are used at a time. Live bait is preferred. When a fish bites, the other liñas are hauled in to avoid *enredinas* (entanglements). Depending on the weight of the fish the struggle to pull it out of the water it may be of long or short duration. Those weighing several hundred kilos may take more than two hours. For skipsack tunas and little tunnys weighing less than 20 kg., a rod with thick casting-line is used.

- The Stone Bass Fishing.- This is one of the most difficult for fishing which requires great knowledge and ability. They are generally found in the deeper waters of the banks, which depth are between 400 and 800 m. The wire line used is strong, resistant, and therefor sensitive, able to transmit the feel of a hit instantly and with full intensity. At the end of this line is strung the *cobrada*: one and a half fathoms (*in spanish called braza*) of thick nylon line with several large hooks. At the end of it, a heavy lead or iron is attached which is named as chumbo. Among fishermen, it is understood the name of fathom as the length of the outstretched arms or a unit of length equal to six feet used especially for measuring the depth of water. Fresh bogues or chub mackerels are used for bait, three or four on each hook, strung through the eyes. The purpose of this type of fishing is to catch stone bass, which can weigh up to 90 kilos, imperial blackfishes, hakes, and several species of sharks are also caught.

- Rock Fishing. By "rock", the fishermen mean to a concrete point down the sea bed, where the concentration of fishes are greatest and the fishing is good. Two forms are practiced: with the boat anchored, or with the boat drifting. The apparatus used is the so-called *cordel* (literally it means line). It consists in a strong nylon line more or less thick -casting line- and at the end, it has several hooks and a lead or steel weight. With the boat anchored the usual catch consists of common sea breams, pink dentex, dusky groupers, comb groupers and others rocky fishes. At night, conger eels, rabbit fishes and oil fishes. White bait is used - squids and sardines, bogues, chub mackerels, and gueldes-. To windward sea, octopus is also used. With the boat drifting, combers and, at night, axillary sea breams are caught.

- The *Palangre* (Boulter).- Basically, it involves a line -la *madre* (literally it means the mother)- from which is hanged down hooks equally in nylon with even

Salemas put to starve.

spaces. At the ends of the line ("the mother") there are two floats or buoys and two *potalas* or *rociegas* (to use as a tool to pull up the boulter). The combined buoy - line - anchor is called a *cabecera*. It is used for fishing common sea breams, pink dentex and fiddle fishes. Squid is the preferred bait, and it is soaked at nightime when the large sea breams come onto the shelf in searching for food. The *palangres* are normally left for two to six hours. The hooks used are small and straight, so that they can be swallowed whole and become lodged deep in the fish's throat or stomach. It is usually picked up at sunrise.

In addition to the species mentioned, a great number of common stingrays and skates are caught. This type of fishing cannot be done in more than 100 m. of subside water.

- Parrot Fish fishing.- It is done from a boat, over a clear bottom, using a rod. The boats used are of small ram and often without motors. The rod feature is provided with a tip made from male goatskin, which increases its sensitivity. A small crab *carnada de vieja* (Xantho Porssa) or *juyón*, biggest crab, are used for baits.

Hunting.
The following is a translation, as we did with the fish section, of some of the regulation for hunting purpose drafted by the Regional Hunting Council at the suggestion of the Sub-committee on Environment.

Hunting season, including the days mentioned, are as follows:

From August 6th to 31st and from October 19th to November 26th , rabbits may be hunted using dogs but no rifles on Thursdays, Sundays and national holidays. The ferret must be with hunting dogs.

From September 3rd to October 15th all authorized species may be hunted using dogs and rifles but only on Sundays and national holidays and on Virgin of Los Dolores holiday, while on Thursday of this period only the rabbit without rifle can be hunted.

The following species can be hunted: red partridge, barbary partridge, quail, turtle dove, rock dove and rabbit.

Hunting is prohibited using compressed air guns, 22 caliber rifles, or any gun with a capacity to hold more than two cartridges at a time. As well, the possession or use of cartridges at a time is prohibited.

The possession or use of decoys with tape recording or animal sounds is prohibited, as is the use of blind or mutilated live decoys, and partridge decoys. A kind of hunting called *cetrería* (hawking) is as well prohibited.

Hunting is prohibited in all wetland areas (ponds, pools, salt marshes, etc.) and within 50 meters of the surrounding areas.

Just to remain that it is illegal to hunt from vehicles or motorboats.

A maximum of five hunters per group, 4 dogs per hunter or 10 per group are permitted. Up to 3 rabbits or 2 quails per hunter and day or 12 pieces, rabbits and quails (with a maximum of 5 quails), per group.

Likewise, hunting is prohibited in Timanfaya National Park, in the place of scientific interest of *Janubio* and the field of urbanisation called "Costa Teguise". Within the *Chinijo* Archipelago Natural Park hunting is allowed in the island of Graciosa, and without rifles in the *Risco de Famara*, from *Rincón de la Paja* to the boundary of *Gusa*. *Llanos de los Ancones*, *El Jable* and the area of *El Rubicón* are considered Reservation Areas, where rabbit hunting is permitted, using no rifle, only on Thursdays, with authorization and control of the Environmental Office Vice-Counsel beforehand; with a maximum of 4 hunters per group, 2 dogs per hunter or 6 dogs per group. A maximum of 3 rabbits per hunter and day and 8 rabbits per group.

The Vice-Counsel Office has the faculty to modify the hunting season period of some or all species with the purpose to support their preservation.

Hunting out of season is considered a serious offense, as well as hunting, illegal possession or commercialization of samples of protected species. Eggs and young shall have, per unit, count for the same as reproducing species.

Perdiz moruna (Barbary Partridge).

PROTECTED NATURAL AREAS

The Canary Islands are a Macaronis archipelago in which its climatic, geologic, marine, geomorphologic, zoological, and botanical characteristics have constituted as a hole an exceptional nature medium. Although, the territory fragmentation, the demographic density, and the almost exclusive dependence of its economy of service areas have generated a type of development impossible to maintain, as the exceeding of recovery capacity of our nature resources are concerning.

This situation demands corrective actions and among them, the establishment of a general legal regulation about the Nature Areas of the Canary Islands. The 12/1994 Act, of December 19th, about Nature Areas of Canary Islands, seeks to be the main instrument that establishes a great social agreement about the Nature and the development, based on the education and consciousness of the environment and through the definition of concrete objects of conservation that force to prevail the purpose in the administrative system which shall guarantee this Act.

The Nature Areas of the Canary Islands Act regulates the arrangement of the nature resources of the archipelago. It determines the different categories of protection and the instruments of planing. It confi-gures a new type of administrative organization. And it establishes a penalty system capable to guarantee the purpose and objectives the Act foresees.

The purpose of this Act is to protect, keep, restore and improve the nature sources and the essential ecology process that take place there, as well as to maintain and restore the landscape that sustain it.

Its objective shall be the methodical use of nature resources, guaranteeing an enduring the development; the integration of those nature spaces which require the conservation or restoration; the promotion of scientific investigation, the environmental education, and the encounter of the man with the nature. All of that should be in a compatible way with the preservation of its values, the improvement of the life quality of local communities bonded to the socio-economic influential areas, and the restoration and recovering of the ecosystems.

The current Act is to be applied to all land and sea territory of the archipelago, so much as the subsoil and the space flown through, without prejudice of the State competence.

Citizens and public authority have the responsibility to respect, keep and repair all damages to them.

According to the nature value and goods that are protected, the Nature Areas are integrated in a

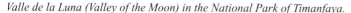

Valle de la Luna (Valley of the Moon) in the National Park of Timanfaya.

System in which the more significant nature habitat and the main bio-diversity centers are represented with the following rank:

- Nature and Rural Parks.
- Nature Reserves: Integral and Specials.
- Nature Monuments.
- Protected Landscapes.
- Places of Scientific Interest.

Nature Parks are those wide-spread Natural Spaces, sensibly untouched by the human exploitation and occupation and such natural beauty, fauna, flora and gea as a hole are considered singular examples of the nature patrimony.

Rural Parks are those wide-spread Natural Spaces in which coexist agricultural, livestock or fishing activities with others of special natural and ecology interest.

The Natural Reserves have as a purpose to protect the ecosystems, communities or biological or geological elements that, due its oddness, fragility, representation, importance or peculiarity deserve a special assessment. As a general rule, the gathering of biologic and geologic materials is prohibited.

Integral Natural Reserves are those of moderate dimension, which purpose is the integral preservation of all of its elements, as well as every natural ecological process.

Special Natural Reserves are those of moderate dimension, which purpose is the preservation of exceptional habitats, concrete species, geologic formation or natural ecological process of special interest.

Nature Monuments are spaces or elements from the nature, with small dimension, basically constituted by formations of evident peculiarities, oddness, or beauty. Specially, the geologic formation, the paleontologic measures, and other elements of the gea that have a special interest due to the singularity or importance of its scientific, cultural or landscaping values.

The Places of Scientific Interest are those natural places, generally isolated and with small dimension. In these places exist natural elements of scientific interest, specimens or animal or plant populations threaten due to extinction or worthy to have specific measures to be preserved.

Likewise of Canary Natural Space network, the Natural Parks exists managed by the Nutrition, Fishing and Agricultural Ministry Department. Those are protected spaces of relative extension, with primitive ecosystem which were not been affected by the human action and where the fauna, flora, and geomorphologic formations have an outstanding cultural, educational-recreational interest or where it exists natural landscape of great beauty.

Natural Spaces of Lanzarote island:

National Park of Timanfaya.

This area was declared Natural Park on August 9th, 1974. The Park Board of Governors was the collaborator organ to manage the park and it is under supervision of the *Plan Rector de Uso y Gestion* (Usage and Management Superior Plan).

It comprises an area of 5,107 hectares, with 30 km. perimeter and 540 m. maximum high. It is located between Yaiza and Tinajo municipal boundary.

The eruption nucleus of 1730-1736 constituted, for this type of eruptions, one of the volcanologic spaces more important in the world. One can observe the greatest different structure varieties in lava and structures. It can be localized more than 25 craters in a reduced area of a few square km.

Likewise, Its great differences with the rest of recent eruptions of the archipelago can attract attention, so in length of time as in volume and composition of lava throw out the surface.

The volcanic eruption of energy and effects in the historical period of the Earth has been incomparably bigger, although of explosive character. The effusive nature, like from Lanzarote island, are characterized by the emission of great quantity of lava through cracks of great growth. The most important eruption in the historic time is Lakagigar, occurred in 1783 in Iceland, followed by Lanzarote with greater length.

These emissions of basaltic magma happened through a 14 km. crack. The lava flow followed noticeable tracks, like *Montaña de las Nueces* (Walnut mountain) next to *Montaña Colorada* (Red mountain) that went 20 km. with an average slope of 2%, penetrating in the sea about 300m. through Castle of San José, next to Arrecife.

The eruptive stages of 1824 that formed the Tinguatón, Tao and Chinero volcanoes (only the latest is located inside of Park), raised as well on a 13,5 km. crack with parallel direction of the one in 1730.

Type of the eruption from 1730-36
- Maximum flow: $4,8 \times 10^6$ cu.m./day.
- Exit speed: 0,27 m/s.
- Theoretical maximum longitude reached by the casting: 12 Km.
- Longitude of well-known casts: 5 to 9 Km.
- Typical height of the cones: 100-200 m.
- Average life of the cones: 10 days.
- Average speed of growth: 10 cu.m./s.

ESPACIOS NATURALES PROTEGIDOS
NATURSCHUTZGEBIETE
PROTECTEC NATURAL SPACES

Parque Nacional de Timanfaya
Timanfaya-Nationalpark
Timanfaya National Park

Parque Natural del Archipiélago Chinijo
Naturpark des Chinijo-Archipels
Archipiélago Chinijo Natural Park

Reserva Natural Integral de los Islotes
Integriertes Naturreservat der Felseninseln
Integral Natural Reserve of the Islands

Parque Natural de los Volcanes
Naturpark der Vulkane
Volcanoes Natural Park

Monumento Natural de La Corona
Naturdenkmal La Corona
Natural Monument of the La Corona

Monumento Natural de los Ajaches
Naturdenkmal Ajaches-Massiv
Ajaches Natural Monument

Monumento Natural de la Cueva de los Naturalistas
Naturdenkmal "Cueva de los Naturalistas"
Natural Monument of the Cueva de los Naturalistas

Monumento Natural del Islote de Halcones
Naturdenkmal "Islote de Halcones"
Natural Monument of Islote de Halcones

Monumento Natural de Montañas del Fuego
Naturdenkmal "Montañas del Fuego"
Natural Monument of Mountain of the Fire

Paisaje Protegido de Tenegüime
Landschaftsschutzgebiet Tenegüime
Protected landscape of Tenegüime

Paisaje Protegido de la Geria
Landschaftsschutzgebiet La Geria

OCEANO ATLANTICO

PUNTA DE JUAN REBENQUE
PUNTA DELGADA
PUNTA GRIETA
LA BERMEJA
PUNTA TRABUCO

ALEGRANZA

ROQUE DEL OESTE

MONTAÑA CLARA
PUNTA DEL AGUA

PUNTA DE LA CAMELLA
PUNTA GORDA
PLAYA DE LAS CONCHAS

PUNTA DE LA SONDA

Pedro Barba

LA GRACIOSA
Caleta del Sebo
EL RIO

PUNTA DEL BAJIO
PUNTA DEL POBRE
PLAYA DEL RISCO

PUNTA DE FARIONES
PLAYA DE LA CANTERIA

Orzola
Mirador del Río
Ye
Guinate
Los Helechos
581
Máguez
HARIA
Tabayesco

LAS BAJAS
PLAYA DE FAMARA

EL CAMPANARIO
ROQUE DEL ESTE

PUNTA DEL PALO
Escamas
214 PUNTA ESCAMAS
JAMEOS DEL AGUA
Cueva de los Verdes
Punta Mujeres
Arrieta

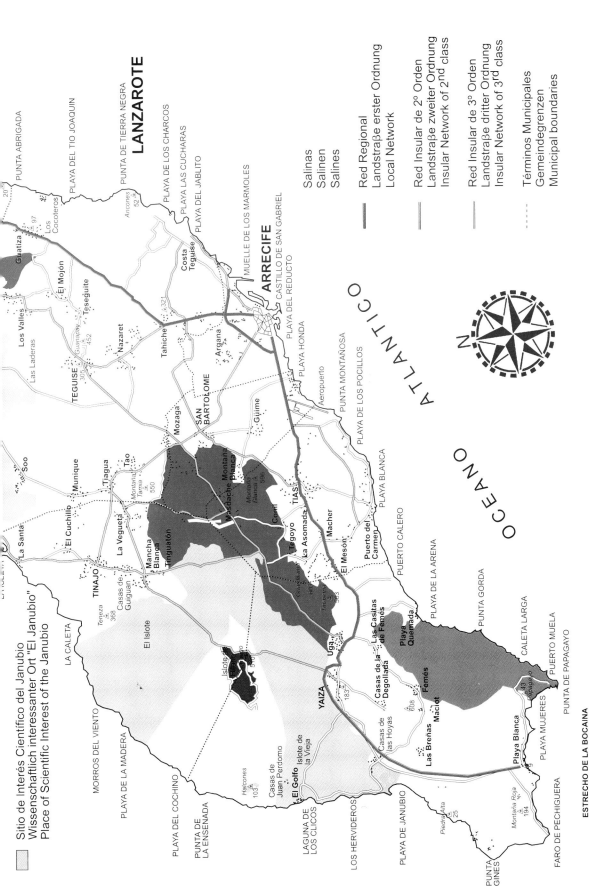

LANZAROTE

ARRECIFE

OCÉANO ATLÁNTICO

Sitio de Interés Científico del Janubio
Wissenschaftlich interessanter Ort "El Janubio"
Place of Scientific Interest of the Janubio

Salinas
Salinen
Salines

Red Regional
Landstraße erster Ordnung
Local Network

Red Insular de 2° Orden
Landstraße zweiter Ordnung
Insular Network of 2nd class

Red Insular de 3° Orden
Landstraße dritter Ordnung
Insular Network of 3rd class

Términos Municipales
Gemeindegrenzen
Municipal boundaries

N

PUNTA ABRIGADA
PLAYA DEL TIO JOAQUIN
PUNTA DE TIERRA NEGRA
PLAYA DE LOS CHARCOS
PLAYA LAS CUCHARAS
PLAYA DEL JABLITO
MUELLE DE LOS MARMOLES
CASTILLO DE SAN GABRIEL
PLAYA DEL REDUCTO
PLAYA HONDA
Aeropuerto
PUNTA MONTAÑOSA
PUNTA DE LOS POCILLOS
PLAYA DE LOS POCILLOS
PLAYA BLANCA
PUERTO CALERO
PLAYA DE LA ARENA
PUNTA GORDA
CALETA LARGA
PUERTO MUELA
PUNTA DE PAPAGAYO
PUNTA DE LA BOCAINA
ESTRECHO DE LA BOCAINA

Guatiza
Los Cocoteros
97
El Mojón
Teseguite
Nazaret
Tahiche
Argana
Costa Teguise
Los Valles
Las Laderas
TEGUISE
305
Guanapay
452
Mozaga
SAN BARTOLOME
Güime
Soo
Munique
Tiagua
Tao
Montaña Tamia 550
La Veguetá
El Cuchillo
La Santa
TINAJO
Teneza 368
Casas de Guiguan
Mancha Blanca
Tinguatón
Masdache
Montaña Blanca 596
Montaña Blanca
Conil
Tegoyo
La Asomada
TIAS
Macher
El Mesón
Puerto del Carmen
Guardilama 603
Atalaya de Femés
MORROS DEL VIENTO
PLAYA DE LA MADERA
PUNTA DE LA ENSENADA
PLAYA DEL COCHINO
LA CALETA
El Islote
Halcones 103
Casas de Juan Perdomo
El Golfo
Islote de la Vieja
183
Uga
LAGUNA DE LOS CLICOS
LOS HERVIDEROS
PLAYA DE JANUBIO
Casas de las Hoyas
Las Casitas de Femés
Playa Quemada
Casas de la Degollada
Femés
Maciot
Las Breñas
YAIZA
Montaña Roja 194
Piedra Alta 25
PUNTA GINES
FARO DE PECHIGUERA
Playa Blanca
PLAYA MUJERES
Papagayo 143
608
El Islote
Muñique
452
321
20
Arcones 52

Caldera Rajada alignment, Montaña Encantada, and Pedro Perico. In a close-up, sunken volcanic tuff.

The main structures as volcanic values are concerning are as follows:

Blowing cone (*in spanish called Hornitos*). Secondary eruptive mouth where lava and gases were expelled without forming a structure of big dimensions. These openings often are located in elementary tunnels which ceiling was deformed due to the constant pressure under the inside lava gases. The most characteristic of the Park is the so-called "*Manto de la Virgen*" (The Virgin shawl).

Volcanic tuff. They are tunnels of several length originated by rivers of underground lava that continue flowing inside after solidification in the surface. When finishing the lava eruptions, the volcanic tuff is formed. After the lava fluid is finished, and since it can resist the materials and the tension originated by the tunnel vault, the ceiling of this tunnel collapses and this causes the hole formation called "*jameos*".

Lava sea. Two different types of lava form mainly this lava sea: ones very consistent and when cooling down a crust is formed, rough and impassable surface known as "*malpaís*", and others more fluid with smooth surface or some roughness in the surface and they are called "*cordadas*".

Cinder Conos (volcanic structures covered in its entirety by eruptive materials of small dimensions (piroclastes. Pyro = fire; claste = fragment) and derive from the latest phase of volcano (stromatolitic phase).

Among the volcanic materials several types, according to dimension, can be recognised:

Ashes. Lava dust in suspension after the eruption (less than 2 mm.).

Lapillus (*brasier charcoal or ballast*). A small stony or glassy fragment of lava thrown out in a volcanic eruption (from 2 to 20 mm.). This material is used in agriculture because of the hygrocospic attributes.

Clinker. Stony matter fused together with irregular shape and quite bigger than Lapillus material. The clinker is used to build the walls that protect the sand-bank.

Blowing cone called "Manto de la Virgen"

34

Volcanic bomb. Round or oval shape due to the turning movement when coming out and falling. Usually they are located close to the craters.

Accretion balls. Huge balls of lava formed in a similar process to the snowing balls falling down the hillside.

Other important characteristics of this volcanic area are the thermal anomalies. These anomalies seem to be associated to the rain system and the activities can be identified easily by the abundance of salty deposits (sulphate) that come along with. The alignment of reeds are good biologic indicator of the geothermal activity. These alignment of reeds are distributed forming a circle of 180° around a thermal anomaly of low temperature. The reed needs a lot of water to a moderate temperature.

In *Hilario* island takes place thermal anomalies that, traditionally, have been used as natural ovens. The temperatures stockings reach up 600° C at 12 m. It is possible to measure 250° C almost reaching the surface.

The tourist attraction of the artificial geysers shows the scarce energy in surface. It is cooled down from 300° to 98° C just with a single bucket of water, taking two hours in recovering. For this reason the use of the soil drilling is alternated. Temperature is about 160° C. in the natural blowing cones while in one of them (where the gorses are burned) temperature up to 400° C. are reached

An important part of lava field is observed from the 1730-36 and of 1824 eruptions (*Nuevo del Fuego* or *Chinero* volcano) from *Hilario* island, as well as the alignment of cones of *Montaña del Fuego, Calderas Quemadas* and *Montaña Rajada*, where thermal anomalies also appear.

In *Montaña Rajada* of very variable character, are detected the latest thermal anomalies, with inferior temperatures up to 150° C. In this structure two almost concentric craters are located which correspond to two differentiated eruptive stages. A lake of lava is located at the bottom of the first crater which overflows from the north side.

From *Montaña Rajada*'s watch tower it is possible to contemplate the whole alignment of cones associated to two parallel geologic fractures.

In the lava sea there is a volcanic tunnel that leaves from the bottom part of this mountain and continuous about 2 km. before joining with another tunnel coming from *Caldera Rajada*'s small cone. The tunnel roof ispartially sunken which allows to follow the track from the watch tower. We can distinguish, in this lava field, a flat lava type called "*cordadas*" and the rough ones called "*malpais*".

Taro de los Camelleros is another point where there are thermal anomalies of lineal character associated to superficial cracks.

Timanfaya is the only crater that presents activity signs. In the observation of plant colonization

Alignment of reeds near Montaña Rajada.

Interior of a cone populated with líchens.

the modifications can be reflected acting as biological indicator. *Pico de Fuego* is the name given from the strong thermal anomalies present in the whole structure. *Caldera de los Cuervos* or the *Corazonci- llo* can be observed from the watch-tower and in a second level *Pico Partido*'s volcanic complex appears, the highest in the series (518 m.), with lake of lava in the crater and variety of tunnels and natural blowing cones.

In the bottom of the *Timanfaya* crater, at 2m. depth, thermal anomalies with 300º C are located. In spite of the temperature and the gassy emissions, communities of lichens exist. The fact that the lichens are receptive to the action of these emanations it is due to the slow growth and the inability of eliminating toxic substances.

Caldera del Corazoncillo is one of the volcánic structure more impressive. It has a deep crater of 137 m. depth in funnel shape and 400 m. diameter, being the lower bottom 33 m. below the bench mark of the lava field. The pyrroclastic hillsides highlight for the chromatism. The formation of this volcano was extremely violent. It corresponds to a sinking boiler and it is possible that some thermal

springs were located in the past since the caldera is found today.

Chinero is the last volcano that arose in this Park giving an origin to a volcanic tunnel which reaches the coast.

This Park possesses a series of facilities and services that will make more suitable and educational your visit. By reaching the Park from Yaiza you will find in first place *"Echadero of the Camellos"*, where the Museum of Rocks and an Information Office are located. There are also a bar, a souvenirs store and toilets, all underground facilities. A trip with camels is offer in this place to travel through the south hillside of the Timanfaya.

Taro de Entrada is located following the highway that leads to the tourist facilities *"Montaña del Fuego"* in *Islote de Hilario*. Restaurant, bar, souvenirs stores, toilets and parking are located in this place. The Park personnel will make you demonstrations on the geothermal anomalies described previously.

From here you can go to the so-called *"Ruta de los Volcanes"* (Route of the Volcanoes). Through a 14 km highway, the more sensational areas of the Park can be crossed. The only way of making this journey possible is in the *"guagua"* (bus) of the Town council. The Visitors and Interpretation Center of Mancha Blanca can be found continuing toward the municipality of Tinajo. This free access center has a permanent exhibition equipped with constructional panels, interactive videos, scale models, scientific instrumental booths, library, as well as an exceptional poly-language audio-visual program.

Other interesting services offered is the "Interpretive Routes" guided on foot through the interior of the Park. This will allow you a deeper contact with the nature. It consists of two itineraries:

Route of *Tremesana*: 3 km. length with an approximate 2 hours duration and a minimum difficulty. In this route you can contemplate so much geologic

Stroll on camels.

aspects as biological. Flow lava, volcanic tuff, bubbles, alignment of cones and craters, the start of vegetable life in a recent floor, as well as cultivation areas are some of the phenomenon that you can observe.

Coast Route. 9 km. length with an approximate 5 hours duration and a half degree of difficulty. This route begins in *Playa de la Madera* along the coast belonging to the National Park. The formation of a recent coast can be noted for the arrival of the lava, *malpaises*, as well as the resurgence of the plants and animal life. We are arriving at *Playa del Cochino,* in the middle of the itinerary, where we will begin our way back. Closed and resistant footwear, provisions of water, and slight food are recommended to take for this route.

As well we recommend the respect of some minimum norms of behavior in order to guarantee the conservation of the fragile landscape: Avoid getting animals, plants, or volcanic stones samples. Prevent from walking outside of the paths and not to throw garbage, brashess or butts during the journeys.

The guided route services are for a group up to 7 people (maximum) and you have to arrange this guide route previously by telephone or personally in the Administrative Offices.

The Administrative Offices are in Tinajo where a visitor information office is located at 64 Laguneta street. Tel.: 84 02 38 or 38 23 40.

Chinijo Archipelago Natural Park.

9.112 hectares extension in the municipal terms of Haría and Teguise.

It is formed by all the islands in the north of Lanzarote (La Graciosa, Alegranza, Montaña Clara, Roque del Este and Roque del Oeste), the fringe of the western coast of the *Famara* massif and *Lomo Blanco*'s plains and *Blanca* coast, including the surrounding sea. A Natural park was declared in 1986, being the first Spain marine-terrestrial natural park.

These two natural units, so different to each other, were integrated due to the high natural values and landscape that converge in the area of contact of these two natural spaces.

The geologic antiquity oscillates between: Series I (Old series or First Volcanic Cycle) like *Famara* and where a long erosive process has taken place; and series III and IV (Recent vulcanism) that include the islands and some points of *Famara*. In past geologic times, all these islands, together with Lanzarote and Fuerteventura, formed a single physical unit due to the regressions of the sea caused by the ice effect in the Glacial epoch.

Riscos of Famara forms an impressive cliff with 500 m. approximately of medium height, 22 km. length and 4 km. wide. The maximum height is *Peñas del Chache* with 670 m. It is a dominant point of the island.

Punta Fariones and cliffs of Famara seen from La Graciosa.

Beach of La Cocina (the Kitchen).

This great volcanic structure is configured by old basalt accumulation with alternated levels of material broken into lava fragments (pyroclastic) and levels of reddish loamy floors called almagres (red earth) which denote periods of volcanic calm. A river of lava appears in the middle north of this cliff which has overflowed from the high part. It comes from the prehistoric eruption of *La Corona*'s volcano. Cliffs of extreme slope that fall to the sea appear in the central part and in the north extreme of the southwest part and north-west plains.

Famara constitutes an important botanical focus not only at the archipelago level but at the world level. In a 6% of the territory is located 75% of Lanzarote endemic flora. Out of the 291 present species inside the park, 19 are insular endemism (14 exclusive of *Famara*), 21 from the oriental islands, 24 canary and 11 macaronesics.

The islands rise on a submarine platform with 100 m. approximately of medium depth. The surface of each one of them is as follows: La Graciosa, 27 sq. km., Alegranza, 11,7 sq. km.; Montaña Clara, 1,12 sq. km.; Roque del Este, 0,71 sq. km.; Roque del Oeste, 0,06 sq. km.

The caldera of *Alegranza* and *Montaña Clara* highlight for their geomorphology as well as the water-magmatic character of *Montaña Amarilla*. After a strong erosive process the internal structure is observed as a spectacular chromatism.

There is less than 1 km. distance from La Graciosa to Lanzarote and they are separated by a sea string denominated *El Río* with 10 m. average depth.

The whole island is almost plain with just few meters above the sea level in which several pyroclastic cones highlight as: *Montaña Bermeja* to the north with 157 m. high; *Montaña Amarilla* to the south with172 m. high; and toward the center, *Montaña del Mojón* with 185 m. high, and the *Pedro Barba* group with 266 m. high which it is the maximum height of the island.

Between these and other smaller elevations some basins appear where fine clays are deposited together with sands that the wind brings from the north-east coast.

The coast is widespread with beaches. In the south are located: *Bahía del Salado, Caletón del Marrajo* and the surprising *Playa de la Cocina* in the hillside of *Montaña Amarilla*. In the north: *Playa Lambra* and *Playa de las Conchas*. The latest is maybe the best beach of the park and Lanzarote.

Important fields of dunes are formed that harbour an unique vegetation inside the park, next to Montaña Bermeja as to Pedro Beard's group in the South. The *balancones* (Traganum moquinii) communities are plentiful and they develop and settle big dunes. The sedge communities are as well

Montaña Clara y Roque del Oeste.

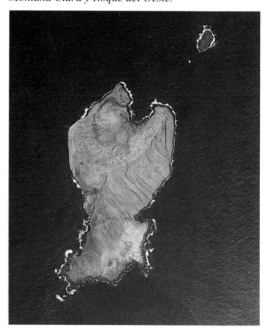

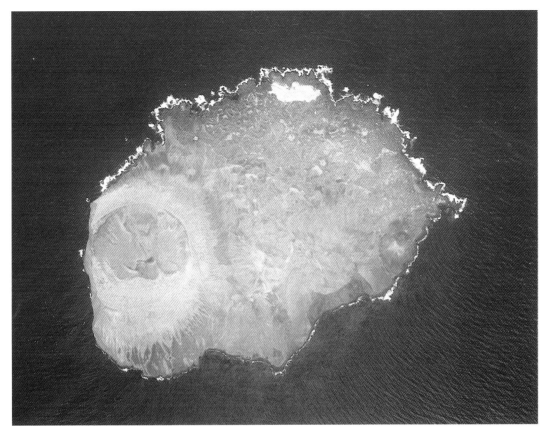

Alegranza.

abundant, characteristic of mobile sands, with more floriferous wealth. And next to these, brushwood varieties that fix small earthy dunes and whose components are floridly diverse.

La Graciosa includes as well remarkable endemism as *corazoncillo de Lanzarote* (lotus lanzarotesi), evergreen (limonium ssp.), or some asparragus variety, among others. Just as the only characteristic endemism of this island, *flor mala* or *florón* (lit. bad flower).

Montaña Clara is located to the North of La Graciosa. Another volcanic cone that appeared on the surface reaching a maximum height of 251 m.

Regarding the geomorphology highlights: An open hillside to the north from where the sea penetrates. The steep west coast reaching 200 m. high. The reddish tonalities of rocks and pyroclasts in which the sea has sculpted caves and natural pools. And a small plain to the south.

The vegetation deserves a special attention since it presents the biggest endemism percentage, so much macaronesics as from Lanzarote -*corazoncillo of Lanzarote*, evergreen, *carallumas* (caralluma

burchardii),...-, having as well its own endemism. The alteration due to introduced species is low.

Alegranza is the most northern point in the Canary archipelago. The most outstanding as geomorphology is concerning is the denominated volcanic structure *La Caldera*. It is located in the most western part of the island. It almost occupies a third part of the island surface. The crater has a 250 m. depth and a 1200 m. diameter. reaching 289 high. The interior walls have a great slope and in the bottom there are sings of old agricultural utility with a reservoir that brings up the waters. Another fascinating place is *Cueva del Jameo*. A deep incoming to the south of *La Caldera*, navigable inside for small boats, until reaching the island again with a distance of 200 m. approximately. The rest of the island is already a platform with some smaller cones dismantled already among those which mix small clay basins.

The vegetation presents similar degradation levels to those of La Graciosa, except in the north part of *La Caldera* where is less altered. The presence of goats and rabbits represent a great threat for this precarious flora. The *furzes* communities and *tabaibas*

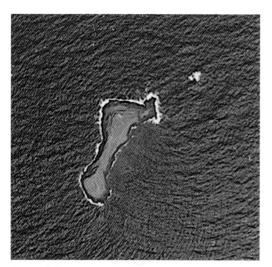

Roque del Este.

(auphorbia) are abundant, and among the existent endemism to highlight the everlasting and the *tajinaste of Lanzarote* (echium handiense) as well as the garlic of Alegranza, exclusive from this island.

El Roque del Oeste is a remaining black lava, in an advanced erosion state, with 40 m. high on the sea level.

And finally, Roque del Este, located at 11 km. far from the east part of Lanzarote. It is the rest of a double peryclasts cone, with reddish colour and very deteriorated by the marine erosion. As curiosity, an underwater tunnel that crosses the island can be pointed out.

The bird fauna of the Natural Park is important and has very diverse origin. It is conditioned by the geographical situation of the park. Located in the Current of the Gulf and in contact with one of the marine areas, as for nutritious, more important of the world. Therefore, the marine birds communities take a suitable place for their nest. Mainly in the islands where a dozen of threatened birds nest. Also a multitude of migratory birds of all Europe go by these islands.

The cory's shearwater (*in spanish called pardelas*) communities are numerous and possibly the biggest of the Canary Islands. Although when the man arrived the pardelas slaughters also began. At the beginning they killed them only to balance the sole fish diet and only a small numbers of samples had a small effect. But at the beginning of this century and for oil purpose the slaughters began up to 12.000 *pardelas* per season. From then on and until few years ago the massacres have continued for what the population's descent has been alarming. Today some 2.000 *pardelas* couples can be counted.

Colonies of species also exist so rare as Bulwer's petrel or the storm petrel and petrel of Madeira.

In the coastal areas we can find limicolas birds besides the omnipresent gull: storne-curlew, little *egret*, etc.

Among the predators highlights the osprey. Bird in regression in the entire world and it counts here with almost half of the couples existent in all Canary. Eleonor's hawk is another small predator and strange which settled down here.

The plains of Soo have a good representation of steppe birds: houbara bustard, cream-colored courser, ...

The terrestrial vertebrates are common in the whole park, highlighting two canary endemic species of reptiles: the Atlantic lizard and the brittle lizard. The latest is in clear extinction danger.

The mammals are scarce. To point out the canary shrew. This endemic species inhabits in Montaña Clara. It is the last mammal species discovered in the world.

Although the human establishments inside the park are located in Caleta del Sebo and Pedro Barba (in La Graciosa) and Caleta de la Villa and the urbanization of Famara (in Lanzarote). The incoming visitor every time is bigger, mainly in summery time.

Another picturesque point to highlight inside the park is the oldest of Canary, *Salinas del Río*, conditioned by Sancho de Herrera, the first gentleman of Lanzarote. The access is easy by small crafts from Caleta de Famara, Orzola and Caleta del Sebo, or on foot by a path that communicates these salt flats with the valley of *Guinate* and *Vega Chica* (near Ye). Being the nearest road between La Graciosa and Lanzarote.

Integral Natural Reserves of the Islands.
Area with 165,2 hectares in the municipality of Teguise. The geographical boundary belongs together with the perimeter, starting from the lines of low tide, of Montaña Clara's islands, Roque del Este and Roque del Infierno or del Oeste; all of them inside the National Park of the Chinijo Archipelago.

They have already been described in the previous section. The difference rests in the type of legal protection. As we said in Natural Parks chapter, the Integral Natural Reservations are those, of moderate dimension whose object is the integral preservation of all their biotic and abiotic elements, as well as all the natural ecological processes.

Natural Park of the Volcanoes.
Covered 10.158,4 hectares in the municipal terms of Tinajo, Yaiza and Tías.

This Park surrounds the National Park of Timanfaya. Most of the surface is fields of lava corresponding to the eruptions of 1730 - 36 and to the eruption of 1824. Although there are also cones belonging to previous series, called islands,.

Lagoon of the Clicos. El Golfo.

Caldera Blanca is one of the cones more characteristic in this Park. It belongs to the series III. It is of clear color and one of those "islands" distributed by the Park. The bottom of the caldera is about 149 m. on the sea level and the more elevated point is on 458 m. That is to say, it has 309 m depth. The circular base has near 2 km. diameter.

To the east *Pico Partido* I and II appear ; two twin picks of 518 and 502 m. high. We could say for sure that the first eruptions of the period of 1730-36 were located in this sector. These volcanoes were destroyed by later explosions and the remains are spread in big blocks in the hillsides.

In the few documents of the eruption of 1730-36 make an appointment repeated times a submarine volcanic activity next to the coast. Only *Montaña del Golfo* represents hydro-volcanism characteristic. At the moment only a part is located from the old structure submitted to a strong erosion. For what it is difficult to reconstruct its original form. This seems to correspond to several emission centers very near. The lagoon of the *Clicos* is inside the crater, with intense green color due to the concentration of a marine alga. This volcano, together with the *Tiguatón* from the eruption of 1824, is the only examples of explosive volcanism in this island.

Big columns of water, with 30 m. high, are observed during the final phase of the eruption of the

El Golfo.

Montaña de las Lapas (Mountain of the Limpets) or El Cuervo (the Crow).

volcano *Nuevo de Tinguatón* since they softened and they enlarged the structure. The most characteristic of this structure is that in the interior a series of circular openings are located, with more than 100 m. depth and aligned according to a fracture. The expelled water in the last phase can be the reason why the conduits have been totally free.

Some tunnels from the 1730-36 eruption reached the west coast where several tuff appear today cut, with a same separation as their diameter.

The predominant vegetation is the lichens, with more than a hundred of present species. Some wild geraniums, *corazoncillos* (lotus lanzarotesi) or endemic *bejeques* of Lanzarote can be seen in these areas. Vineyards and some dispersed fig are located in the areas where the man has intervened.

The few invertebrate existent are forced to feed from the floating plactom to survive, such it is the case of the two endemic scarabs.

The bird fauna is the same one as in other parks.

Natural Monument of La Coro-

na. Covered 1,797.2 hectares in the municipal area of Haría.

The eruptive process that affected the north of the island few thousands years ago (from 3 to 5 millennia) also corresponds to a fissure mechanism of some few emission centers distributed though 5 km. It is the normal type of eruption in the Canary Islands, the same as the chemical composition of the lava that corresponds to a basaltic mineral (green vitriol).

These eruptions usually have, two exit holes: one from where the lava goes out which usually are external cracks; and other, from where the gases together with the ashes, bombs, and other projection materials get out.

The volcano of *La Corona*, arisen with a little more than 200 m. high from the platform of *Guatifay.* Next to the cliff of *Famara* it culminates together with 609 m. on the sea level. It has a diameter of 1,100 m. on the base and 450 m. in the highest part. The bottom of the crater has 190 m. depression from the superior borders.

The plutonic activity of this volcano modifies substantially the orography of the island. The lava ejected in different directions and the eruption should be one of those more spectacular of Lanzarote. The crater is formed by scum and sticky lava thrown in successive explosions with moderate intensity.

Lava is abundant in blocks in the north area. One of the lava string is 400 m. long going through the cliff of *Famara*, reaching the sea to the foot of the cliff. Due to the lava, the sea went backwards 2.500 m in the oriental hillside of the island, occupying a surface of 30 sq. km. between the village of Orzola and the Port of Arrieta. Area that we know as the *Malpaís de la Corona.*

The lava fused the materials through the slope. Also it built a deep channel that when the upper part solidified, a cover was made up with a group of volcanic tunnels that extend up to 7 km long from the emerging volcano until penetrating in the sea about 2 kms. in form of submarine cave. The volcanic tuff of section and moderate longitude are frequent in Canary. But it is in Lanzarote where these tuffs have extraordinary dimensions (*La Cueva de los Natura-listas* and *La Cueva de los Verdes*). As for dimensions is concerning a similar formation doesn't exist in the rest of the planet.

Malpais of La Corona, with Cueva de los Verdes (Cave of the Green) and the volcano of La Corona at the back.

The basaltic rocks are characterized to have a coefficient of calorific conductivity and a specified heat sufficiently low that allows the lava to run under a surface already cooled, protecting it from a quick cooling.

Cueva de los Verdes with hardly one kilometer long , is a route pertaining to this group of tunnels conditioned to be visited. It allows a good approach to the knowledge of the lava flow through these volcanic tuffs. Further, the series of tunnels superimposed with interior vertical connections can be observed. In some points these tunnels end up having three levels and the height of the tunnel can reach 50 m., with 15 m. width. As the one denominated "Conferences Room" were up to 500 armchairs can be placed for that purpose. It presents some exceptional acoustic conditions. The natural ventilation is mild and the interior temperature is uniform, about 19° C.

Besides the spectacular formations and internal structures (lava channels, dragged blocks, drops of lava, salt flats deposits, coloration, etc.), it is important to observe the numerous erosion examples that appear in the internal walls of the tunnel. Like the independent small lava flows, as well as the notable difference in the superficial aspect of the solidified lava inside the tunnel. This happen when ceasing the eruption and the similar materials spilled in the exterior.

Regarding the aesthetic aspect, it is interesting the range of colors of some parts of the vault and the walls. The alive red colors are due to the oxidation of the content in iron of the basalt. The other colorations correspond to the numerous salt flats precipitations that cover the walls for evaporation of the water filtered from the surface.

At historical level, the *Cueva de los Verdes* has served as refuge in the successive pirate invasions that razed the island.

The *jameos* are others in the constructive ways to highlight in these calderas. Among the more important *jameos* figure: *Jameos del Agua, Jameo de los Lagos, Jameo de los Verdes, Jameo de la Puerta Falsa, Jameo Redondo, Jameo de la Gente* and *Jameos de Arriba.*

Detail from the interior of Cueva de los Verdes.

In the wide coast located these lava flow, some natural pools have been formed as *Caletón Blanco, Caletón del Charco,* or *Caletón de la Condesa.*

Lichens and *tabaibas* (auphorbia) are the predominant vegetation. Some specific vegetable species from this sand-bank live in some deposits of sand located in the coast, as the *balancón* (Traganum moquinii) and the *lecheruela* (euphorbia paralias linneo) among others.

The fauna is similar to the rest of the island, although it is to stand out the one that has its habitat inside the *Jameos del Agua* (we will talk about it later on).

Natural Monument of Los Ajaches. 3.009,5 hectares in the municipal term of Yaiza.

They are old geologic mountain formations corroded by the erosion. They correspond to the first terrestrial blooming of Lanzarote (Serie I), with jolting blooming (of volcanic rock) dispersed to the south and more recent eruptive processes (Series II) in *Montaña Bermeja.*

Atalaya de Femés (608 m.) is the most dominant point of the massif. It is a volcanic cone with a rounded summit. It has an approximate age between 15.5 and 13.5 m. yrs. Although it is outside of the protected area. It is one of the *Ajaches* more

characteristic points. *Hacha Grande* (561 m) is located inside this area. And finishing this series we can located *Montaña de la Breña Chica.* From here the hillside descends toward the south, with certain harshness, until a stony plain of soft relief culminating in *Punta de Papagayo.*

The east coast is steep and it harbours some fossil beaches. In the south part it is more gentle and some of the more active and attractive beaches of Lanzarote are located here as: *Papagayo, Playa Mujeres, El Pozo,* etc. For this reason a large number of vehicles run around this area and when being left the track, they cause serious destruction to the ephemeral existent vegetation.

Furzes and some gramineous are the predominant vegetation in the whole protected space since it is not very varied. The same as with the fauna. The goat is the dominant mammal due to the excessive shepherding in the area. The cory´s shearwater is the bird more common with some colonies in the east coast. Kestrels, some hawks and rarely Egyptian vulture, petrels, common tern, or ospreys can also be observed.

Natural Monument of La Cueva de Los Naturalistas. 1.600 m. extension of underground gallery, and 2.1 hectares of surface in the municipal terms of Tías and Tinajo.

South slope of Los Ajaches.

Lake of lava near La Cueva de Los Naturalistas.

This volcanic tuff is one of the singular points of Lanzarote. It is located in a great lake of lava formed by the *Tizalaya* volcano. It is perfectly passable (with the due cautions), and it has characteristic structures of this type of cavities: fronts of lava rivers, lateral terraces and curious staphyli formations (solidified drops of lava in form of clusters).

Juan Bello Mountain, a caldera of 436 m high emerged from a lapillus field and open to the west.

All this group represents one of the most spectacular landscapes of Lanzarote, besides the vineyards planted in the cracks on the side of lava in

the surroundings of the volcanic tuff. They are located at some hundred of meters from Masdache, in direction to Tinajo.

No fauna neither flora is found in the interior of the Cave. The only one that can be concentrated is in the entrances. Extensive communities of lichens and good representation of *bejeques* are found in the surrounding fields of lava.

Natural Monument of Islote de Halcones.

Total of 10,6 hectares in the municipality of Yaiza, inside the Natural Park of Timanfaya. The perimeter surrounds the Island completely, being adjusted to the contact of historical basaltic calderas with the oldest materials not buried by them.

It is a caldera of 104 m. high, with a horseshoe shape formed by old materials (Series III) in an advanced erosion state. It is of reddish tonality.

The study of these islands is of great importance as for its biology is concerning. The species which were not buried by the lava of the Timanfaya are still alive. These species are important since they have followed their evolution separated from any external influence. It can be studied this particular evaluation and the degree of colonization of the surrounding lava. They have become genetic centers in a state of difficult development.

Halcones Islet.

47

As for the plant population of this island, 90 different species have been counted from among those that highlight, for their abundance, furzes and sweet *tabaibas* that cover the hillsides oriented to the north.

The scarab is the more representative fauna.

The access to this place is restricted and it is only possible under authorization of the Administration of the Natural Park of Timanfaya.

Natural Monument of Montañas del Fuego.

An extension of 392,5 hectares in the municipal terms of Yaiza and Tinajo.

It is the central part, and the highest of the Natural Park of Timanfaya. Among the more important points *Montaña de Fuego, Montaña Timanfaya* and the Island of *Hilario* (where the restaurant is located) are included. It represents the fourth eruptive phase of the whole complex starting from 1732. Island of Hilario is the only sample of old materials.

Since the location is inside the N. P. has already been broadly described previously by what we remit you to this section.

Tenegüime Protected landscape.

An extension of 421,1 hectares in the municipal terms of Teguise and Haría. The protection purpose is the ravine landscape. Scarce longitude, only 4 km. It starts from the peak of *Famara* Old Massif, next to the *Peñas del Chache*, being developed in direction NW-SE. It should be grouped together with the Valley of *Temisa* and the *Palomo* Valley as a landscape unit. They are dug ravines in old materials from Serie I.

A series of remodelling have been found in the periphery of the massif with the emergence of volcanoes from Series II and III along the coast. These remodelling have caused the plugging up of the ravines in the way out to the sea. As the formation of basins have taken place where sediments are accumulated. An interesting process of landscape evolution can be observed thanks to the opening of new basins that cut the obstacles.

Beside *Risco de Famara*, the most abrupt relief of the island is found here, being conserved an interesting natural patrimony especially faunistic. A number of 95 species have been found in this place, out of 34 are vertebrate, prevailing the birds with 25 species; representing 75% of the ones that nest in the island. To highlight: The cory's shearwater, in a non coast surroundings. The monochromatic marlet, in non humanized areas, and the common owl. Also to stand out the presence of birds in extinction danger like the guirre and other predators as the Berberia's hawks.

From the floristic point of view, the presence of certain endemism of great interest highlights. However the majority of this space is been colonized

High area of Barranco de Tenegüime (Ravine of Tenegüime).

by communities of substitution due to the intense use of agriculture which were subjected in last times. The presence of relatively evolved floors and protected areas from the wind and the insolation allows the vegetation development of arboreal presence.

The presence of water in the ravine basin during good part of the year and the easy access allowed the aboriginal population's establishment. Very few testimonies have arrived from this presence due to the great work of later agricultural transformation.

The isolation has allowed the life of a traditional agricultural landscape, although enough altered by the action of the time and the elements. The man's action is perceptible in everywhere. It is expressed in an austere landscape in which the natural elements from the landscape are integrated and the transforming actions has great harmony and ethnographic value.

The rudimentary hydraulics works are good example as to take advantage of the scarce rain. Stone walls are built in the basins of the ravines to form small terraces, calls *nateros*. These have for mission to impede the deterioration of the main ravine from the avalanches of water. Also The *nateros* channels the water to biggest terraces in the bottom of the ravine, called *gavias*, to be planted.

Protected Landscape of La Geria.

It constitutes 5.255,4 hectares in the municipal terms of Tinajo, Yaiza, Tías, San Bartolomé and Teguise. The traditional agrarian landscape is the purpose for protection.

To fight against the lack of water and the strong wind, the popular agriculture of Lanzarote has developed an own technology based on the properties of the piroclasts. The free surface cools down at night favouring a great condensation. In this way, retained water in the pores is filtered. During the day, only the free surface is subject to evaporation since the heat hardly penetrates in the ground. The technique consists on the construction of stone walls by way of barrier protectors, generally open to facilitate the access against the wind,. Both objectives are successful in *La Geria*'s typical vineyards, where the grapevines are cultivated in holes in the lapillus, so that the roots can reach the fertile floor.

This type of agriculture requires a long series of processes: To clean the area, to bring arable floor from other points of the island, to cover them of ashy and to build the walls. The lapillus of better quality for this use is the most recent.

The protected area is located in the geographical center of Lanzarote and it is occupied in great majority by the 1730-36 lava.

La Geria.

To highlight important calderas as: *Montaña Chupadero, Guardilama* (603 m.), *Tinasoria* (503), *Montaña Negra, Caldera Colorada, Montaña Blanca* (596 m.), *Guatisea* and *Montaña Tizalaya* (it forms a field of stratum lava with big plates of a great lanscape value).

Besides the cultivated vegetation, the populations of the endemic *bejeque* of Lanzarote highlight.

It is also good to highlight the endemic cricket as representative of the invertebrate fauna.

Place of Scientific Interest of Los Jameos.

It covers 30,9 hectares in the municipal term of Haría. The underground aquatic habitat and concretely the species that inhabit in there are the main purpose for protection.

Jameos del Agua volcanic tuff is very complex regarding the shape as the structure.

Malpaís de la Corona already had its current aspect when a great flow of lava began to arise for the oriental base of the volcano which was collapsing in the clinker and previously poured rocks. This river of lava was opening a deep track where the surface went cooling down and being formed a stable and consistent vault.

The ascents and descents of the lava level have allowed the formation of lateral cornices, corridors, wells, tunnels, and superimposed bridges. Close to the coast these sways of lava cause the instantaneous gasification of the salted water and as consequence big explosions broke the superior vault as it happened in *Jameo Trasero*, the nearest to the coast.

This phenomenon also took place in *Jameo del Agua*. In some points and mainly in a great block that remains next to the hole where it was pulled up is observed clearly.

The protected area is last tract of this great tuff and it includes: *Jameos del Agua, Jameos de los Lagos, Jameo Trasero* and part of the tunnel of the Atlantis (Cavities with lakes of marine water that harbor a characteristic fauna). It is the habitat of a dozen of strange and endemic species, some of which are, also, exclusive of these lakes: *Rimípedo* or blind *Poliqueto*.

Blind crab or *"jameito"* is the most popular species from these jameos. It has become in the animal symbol of Lanzarote. This species has been also found in areas of similar characteristic as in Orzola and El Hierro island. So a dispersion possibility in the ocean is deduced. About 150 of these crab species for square meter complete the vital cycle and maintain their biggest density in the waters of the jameos. This species is similar to the abyssal fauna marine; with white color and has no eyes. There are similar crabs in the marine depths surrounding the Canary Islands, as well as in the Pacific and other points of the Atlantic.

Interior lake of Jameos del Agua.

Bacterium from surroundings of the submarine volcanic fumaroles is the basic food for this specie.

From 1966, *Jameos del Agua* are open to the public. It has restaurant, bar, pool and an auditory with capacity for 500 people. Everything adorned with exuberant and exotic plants as well as plants from the country.

Next to the *jameos* the House of the Volcanoes has been built where the geologic evolution of Lanzarote is exposed.

Janubio Scientific Interest Place.

It covers 168,6 hectares in the municipal term of Yaiza. The halophilous habitat and the associate species, as well as the traditional activity from obtaining salt as it is practiced today are the protection purpose.

The best port in Lanzarote was located in this area and it was razed by the lava from the eruptions of 1730-36. A sand-bar was formed, as well as closing an internal lagoon called *Caleta del Janubio*.

This lagoon is the main refuge and the last of the island for limícolas birds. Some are migratory as the dunlin, and the turnstone. Other net here as the black-footed plover a threatened species.

The lagoon presents a green color, the same as the lagoon of the *Clicos* in the *Golfo*. That is due to the concentration of a marine alga: *Ruppia maritima*.

Great part of the *Janubio* area are nowadays some salt flats. Out 60 salt flats from the XVII century in Canary, 24 were located in Lanzarote, being the *Janubio*'s the biggest, with approximately 500.000 sq. m. Today, we can see only in operation 9 of them. Those in the *Janubio* are being restored entirely, forming one of the most personal landscapes from Lanzarote. The man's genius is represented as the obtaining of the salt; product with a wide range of purposes from the beginning of the new civilizations.

In the industrial archaeological Architecture section we expose the salt production process thoroughly as well as the diversity of Lanzarote types of salt flats.

The protected space also includes: several lime ovens used in the construction for the salt flats; five mills to bring the inundated water to the channels; and several constructions associated to the salt exploitation.

The black sand-bar is composed by arid of basaltic nature on a volcanic platform. Here a beach of beautiful contrasts with the white of the waves can be observed.

The surrounding vegetation is composed by dispersed bushes as furzes, *brusca* (salsona longifolia) and *coscos* (Mesembryanthemum nodiflorum). Although lichens of a whitish color prevails fundamentally.

Salt flats of the Janubio with a lagoon to the back.

HISTORY AND CULTURE

Prehistory. The reasons at some points, why Lanzarote continues to be unknown from the archaeological point of view are as follows: Non digging ore deposits; lost cultural vestiges or buried it under new settlements; old materials used in new constructions; lost of an important part of the archaeological as consequence of the volcanic eruptions that took place in the island in the first half of the XVIII century; and the storms of *jable* in XIX century (1825).

This combination of factors had caused that areas with an extraordinary richness from the archaeological point of view, like *Llanura Central* or *Gran Aldea*, indigenous settlement located in the existent Teguise, have a great difficulty to recovering as a source of information about the first inhabitants of the island.

The first documents about the island are written by the Bontiner and Le Venier monks who were accompanying to the conquerors in the year of 1402. More than a source of information about the pre-European culture actual at that time, are a "song to the hero" who made the conquer possible.

In any case, clarifying the great questions -Who were they?, Where did they come from?, What did they do?- it is something that, with better or less fortune, we have been trying since XVI and XVII centuries. Initially with the first General Histories written by Alonso Espinosa, Leonardo Torriani and Abreu Galindo. J. de Viera y Clavijo tried, with his History of Canary Islands, to give a vision of the first inhabitants. According to this historian, the Archipelago inhabitants were descendants of the former inhabitants of the Atlantis, theory that trying to grant the most legendary and high lineage to these inhabitants.

The continuing coming of the settlement seems happened in a greatly dilated chronological period. Some authors, like Schiwidetzsky, who started from anthropologic studies of European settlements, consider that the islands settlements happened within two stages, overlapping the most ancient with a certain cromañoide human -wide and rugged face and more stocky body-, while the second stage replies to a mediterranoide human type -taller and thinner and fragile and high face-. From a cultural point of view, the latest was more developed.

The most recent theories close to this century (about the origin and settlement of the Canary archipelago) point out with no doubt to a north-African origin. These theories admit that the provenience area of the former inhabitants were the Berber Margery and Saharan framework, but with limits extended from Tunes to Atlantic coast, and from the Mediterranean to sub-Saharan desert. Concretely in the island of Lanzarote was been found remains of partial excavated houses similar to the ones in Morocco or in some areas of Tunes territory, as well as idols of similar stylistic symbolism with the Saharan zoomorphycal sculptures. Also, the found ceramic, so its form as its ornaments used by the former inhabitants, have similitude with the characteristic dishes from this period.

The progressive desertisation of the Sahara, as well as the political problems in the north of Africa during the first millennium before Christ, seems to be the causes for arriving of some conquers to the island. Because of the winds and marine currents, the travel between the island was very difficult and these conquers (with their primitive means of navigation) were unable to return home. Likewise, the number of people who could land at once or in several times is unknown. In any case, the dimension of the conquest might be enough to allow the reproduction up to the date of the conquest.

The missing anthropological studies in Lanzarote, due in some extent by the missing of human remains, prevents from knowing the physical characteristics of their former inhabitants: *majos*. A chronic doesn't exist to clarify how was the settlement in the territory. The remains found in the burial of *Montaña de la Mina* in San Bartolomé, belongs to a north African Mediterranean settlement type and they show a great strength and a high stature.

As well, they present similar characteristics with the found human types in several sepulchral coves of Gran Canaria, and in a proto-historic and Punic graveyard in the Argelia area.

According to Bontier and Le Verrier quotation: "The language of this country looks like very much to the Canary country", the *majos* language is written within the framework of the Libico-Berber language, extended through the north of Africa. Even though alphabetical form inscriptions of difficult classification also have been found: Latin type exclusive from Lanzarote and Fuerteventura, without equivalence in the rest of the Archipelago.

In this sense, the term *guanche*, applied in general to the aborigine of Canary, would reflect a mixture of settlements -Mediterranean, north African and black population- coming from several immigration, and arrived in the island, maybe, one thousand years before this era (B. C.).

Thanks to the latest investigations, we know a little bit more about the culture of these settlements; houses, economy and in general their life style. We know that the settlements were implemented according to the weather conditions, to the land fertility and to the strategic location. These settlements were oriented

Archaeological location in Zonzamas.

in such manner that the growing, pasture, herd and the movements of the neighbouring tribes were able to be seen from there. The Lanzarote habitat type seems to belong to a surface settlement, some were excavated in a ground of volcanic nature. This habitat was grouped in villages but the habitat living in coves was known. Due to the water shortage, a peculiar element called *maretas* turned up to be a device excavated in the ground for water storage.

The aboriginal economy was based on the farming and livestock activities, supplementing with the recollection tasks of wild plant species as well as fishing and shell-fishing.

The production organization, as well as the work division and the forms of land and livestock properties, turns around the family; being the polyandry (each woman had several husbands) a characteristic element of this organization. The land property belonged to the community.

Regarding their "technology", the *tafiages* (cutting utensil made with stone) is the more outstanding.

The ceramic with half-sphere, oval shape and cylindrical tendency and flat base, and as a general rule, with ochre tonality, brown and reddish, presenting in same cases, cutting decoration and geometrical motif in its edges. The clay was mixed with ashes, milled shelves and vegetables.

Lastly, it is possible that their rituals were satisfied and associated with pouring milk on the peak of mountains, as assured by Abreu Calindo in his book, *Historia de la Conquista de las Siete Islas de Canarias* (History of the Conquest of the Seven Canary Islands): "They worshipped to a God, raising their hands up the sky. They made sacrifices in the mountains, pouring with glasses goat milk, called *gánicas*, made by clay".

The aboriginal settlements are all over the island. *Malpaís de La Corona* constituted a well defined area, including some surroundings: like *Bajo del Risco*, a settlement with permanent character; the ravines and the north valley; the plain area of Guatiza-Tahiche seashore, with use of natural coves and rocky outcroppings; the central area of *El jable*; the archaeological area of *Zonzamas*, nowadays (object to be studied) and includes coves, architectonic structures and rupestrine engravings; and finally, the rocky plains in the south, where more than 100 artificial structures of dried stone are counted with a peculiar distribution of the land.

The area of the *El jable* can be considered as a African "link" more characteristic of the island. Its history covers from the initial settlement, long period occupied by the *majos*, until its repopulating by important contingents of Moorish slaves captured in the neighbouring Saharan coast. The archaeological manifestations in the jable were buried by the sandy storm of 1825 where the jable was extended almost to the present boundaries.

The conquest.

From the time the Ancient World finished and happened the Conquest - sometimes even from the mythological world- always the Canary islands information will continue on. Plutarco, Plinio el Viejo or Ptolomeo have talked about these islands.

The Arabs , according to some historians, came to these islands in the year of 956 and 1013 a. C.

In any case, it's sure that Moorish and Christians knew about the existence, even it is probably they have visited these island more frequently than it is recorded.

What it is known for sure is that from the end of the XIII century, the islands started being visited with relative frequency by the European sailors. Technical progress like the compass, compass-card, as well as portolanos and more precise sea charts, would take an extraordinary effort to the sailing technique.

Two previous stages are defined before the final Conquest: One would take the XIV century entirely, with sporadic journeys and with searching of slaves; and the second, already into the XV century, in which the conquest and the occupation of the islands start, finally joining the castillian crown.

Even though we don't have too much information, it seems that a Genoese, called Lancelotto Malocello, established in Lanzarote island in 1312 -as his name comes from-, stayed in this island for a period of twenty years, and being deported finally by the indigenous.

An expedition, organized by Italians and Portugueses in the year of 1341, sponsored by king Alfonso IV of Portugal, whose technical management was at the expense of Nicoloso da Recco and Angiolino de Teggia. This would later be the cause of conflict between the above-mentioned kind and Alfonso XI of Castile, who claimed the Canary Islands since it pertained to the Mauritania Tingitana, domain of the Visigoth, which the Castilian kings understood to be the inheritors.

The Castilian king defended the same argument when in 1344. Through the bulla *"Tua Devotionis Sinceritas"*, Clemente VI Pope appointed Don Luis de la Cerda (sub-treasurer of the government of Castile and member of the embassy of the French king in the papal head office of Avignon) to be the sovereign of the islands. This fact was the cause for Pedro IV of Aragon to enter in a conflict whom D. Luis de la Cerda, self-appointed as Fortune Prince, recurred to ask for financial help.

Before the end of XIV century and according to Pedro de Ayala, in his chronicle of the king Don Enrique III, a new expedition happened, this time by Castilians and one hundred fifty natives were captured to be sold later on as slaves.

But the final conquest and subsequent colonization was not leaded off until the XV century, once the possibilities, so the economic as the strategic, were known of the Archipelago.

This conquest was neither fast nor continuos and it would have ups and downs throughout the entire XV century. The Normans, Jean de Bethencourt and Gadifer de la Salle started this conquest, both subjects of the king of France. But once the conquest started, in the year of 1402, applied to the castilian court to bring debate to the monarch Enrique III, recognizing in this way the Castilian sovereign power above the Canary archipelago.

The first contact taken was within the island of Lanzarote, in summer of 1402, where friendship agreement with the aboriginal chief took place. The first Norman settlement, named Castillo de Rubicón, was raised in the south of the island.

While Jean de Bethencourt, needy of economic and men support, returned to the Peninsula, Gadifer started a recognition through the rest of the Archipelago, disembarking first in Gran Canaria, going through the coast of Tenerife and later on penetrating into La Gomera and El Hierro islands. Bethencourt came back with a title of king of Canary.

The Norman stage finished in the year of 1418 when Conde de Niebla seized with the rights of the islands. Then, the substitution of the Norman laws for the ones of the Castilian kingdom started.

In 1420, a conflict was raised when king Juan II of Castile donated the islands to Alfonso de Las Casas. No solution was found until 1430, year when Conde de Niebla give the insular rights to Guillén de las Casas, heir of Alfonso de las Casas.

The conflict begins again between Castile and Portugal on the interests that both powers try to maintain with Canary Islands. This conflict was created in the Kingdom of Castile by the ownership of the Archipelago and due to the interests which Portugal continues maintaining in the African continent. This interest was created when giving king Duarte the rights of Portugal to his brother, prince Enrique.

This conflict will last almost one century before Foreign jurists, the papacy and, successively the Castilian kings Juan II, Enrique IV and the Catholic Kings intervene to resolve it. It finishes finally with the treaty of Alcazovar signed in the year 1479, with the victory in favor to the Catholic Kings.

In 1494, soon after the discovery of America, the frontiers would be settled down again -by means of Tordesilla treaties-, and therefore the conquest and colonization rights corresponding to each Kingdom.

Without a doubt, the conquest and colonization of the islands on the part of the Castilian crown, suppose the destruction of the aboriginal world. A new language, a new economy, a new politic, a new culture will substitute the old ones already settled in the archipelago. The considerable decrease of the autochthonous population is the result of illnesses, the slavery, the deportations, the recruitment for the conquest of the other islands, and the difficulty of adapting to a new society, to a new form of life.

The new society will be formed by the aristocracy, the church and the merchants in the high class, small shop owners, artisans, journeymen, enslaved or free aboriginal, black and Moorish captured in the north of Africa will belong to the low class. In sum, an already characterized society for the miscegenation was established.

The Canary archipelago will become the center of pirates and corsairs' attention when the interest of the European powers, guided now toward the American continent change direction. In such a way, from 1515, approximately, the whole marine traffic of the area, will already be seen constantly threatened.

The French pirate Jean Fleury will occupy the island of the Gomera in 1525, due to the conflict created between Emperor Carlos V and the French king. Later on already with Felipe's II reign, the pirates and English corsairs, or the Dutch allies maintained the Archipelago in constant danger, as result of the confrontation between the Spanish king and the queen Isabel I from England.

To preserve their interests, a plan of strengths in the islands will be established by the Spanish monarchy -Carlos V and Felipe II- to recompose the institutions, so much civil as military.

During Felipe III, Felipe IV and Carlos II reigns, the islands are relegated to a secondary level as international politic is concerning, until the arrival of the Borbones in the XVIII century.

It is during Felipe's III reign when the Berber invasions are more intensified. Such invasions were promoted by the expulsion of the Moorish out the peninsula and the alliances of Xerife of Fez with Algerian and Turks. Viera and Clavijo relate us this invasion: "...a Berber and Turk fleets made up of 60 vessels sent by Tabán Arráez and Solimán. 5,000 men disembarked on May 1st of 1618...». The Algerian invaders disembarked without opposition in Arrecife and they went toward Teguise. «...it was taken over on the 2nd and they entered to looting, without the inhabitants found another defense except escaping ...», «...they left toward inland and others didn't stop until being transported to Fuerteventura...». Most of the population hid in *Cueva de los Verdes*, and since

unable to subsist many days they were captured. The invaders abandoned the island with a thousand of captive and a substantial booty. «...this fatal situation left amazed and with tears to Lanzarote. It was good to impoverish the country...». This is the biggest invasion that the island suffered.

Modern history. For different causes (political, economic or natural), Lanzarote is subjected to a period of decadence during the XVI and XVII centuries.

This town have been marked deeply due to natural catastrophes occurred in recent history. Besides the volcanic eruptions, the droughts and the storms, another series of provoked catastrophes as epidemics, wars and invasions, have taken to the population to the emigration and hunger.

In 1730 the island had 4,967 people and the economy, based on the agriculture and the cattle raising, was enough balance. The surface that later covered the lava it was a fertile area, where sources and shepherding areas existed. This part of the island was relatively populated, with some 300 occupied houses.

The maximum civil authority was the Mayor, clerk of the Real Audience with headquarters in Gran Canaria. The maximum military authority was a Sergeant or military Governor who received orders from the Canary Governor in Tenerife. In that moment, Spain, reigned by Felipe V, had a deep crisis since a war was maintained with England and Italy.

The effects of the volcanic eruptions were catastrophic, as it is explained in the stories of that time. The drastic reduction of the subsistence resources originated big trouble for the inhabitants in the following years. Although the long term of the phenomenon and a relative low danger allowed the population to finish getting used and cohabiting with the volcanoes.

We have two different stories from that time: one from Board of Lanzarote and the other from priest of Yaiza. The most precise information is picked up from the legacy of documents mentioned (in the first place) and found in Simancas Registry. These cover up to April 4th 1731. The newspaper of the priest of Yaiza reaches up to December 28th. But it is starting from February of this same year when the story becomes less precise and with dramatic characters. This moment coincides with the worsening of the eruption entering in a second phase with the activity of a new eruptive center: Montañas del Señalo.

The Andrés Lorenzo Curbelo's story (priest of Yaiza), in newspaper form, is without a doubt the better known one: "September 1st of 1730, between 9 h. and 10 h. at night, the earth opened up suddenly close to *Timanfaya*, to two league (approx. 11,145 km.) from

«... a new volcano rose. Ashy and lightnings ejected from the open crater...».

Yaiza, and an enormous mountain rose from the womb of the earth and flames escaped from the apex that continued afire during nineteen days...» And it continues: "...Few days later a new abyss was formed and a torrent of lava threw on Timanfaya, on Rodeo, and on an area of Mancha Blanca. The lava extended on areas toward the North. At the beginning with as much speed as the water. But very soon the speed decreased and the lava run as honey...» And it still continues: "...September 11th the eruption was renewed with more force and the lava ran again. From Sta. Catalina it threw on Mazo. It set on fire and covered this place. Later continued until reaching the sea. Running six days, it followed with an awful noise and forming true waterfalls. A great quantity of dead fish floated in the surface of the sea waters or they came to die to the bank. Suddenly everything calmed down and the eruption seemed to have ceased completely...»

This is the story of the first volcanic episode which lasted 19 days. After a period of rest, 21 to 29 days (not very precise), the volcanic activity is renewed, as the Board of Lanzarote reminds us: "...exploding again on October 10th two mouths, distant only a musket shot from each other and both one third of league from the first volcano...». The priest of Yaiza tells us: "...The inhabitants from Yaiza were forced more than once to escape. The darkness taken place by the amount of ashes and the smoke covering the island were the reason. Up to October 28th 1730 the volcanic action was developed in this way during ten whole days. The livestock died at once suffocated in the whole district by a development of pestilent vapours condensed and falling in form of drops...» It was emanations of sulfurous gases (possibly SO_2) and mainly CO, this last one heavier than the air. It accumulates in the lowest areas, killing for asphyxia to animals of short size, without affecting people on foot or by horse.

The story of this phenomenon in the documents of the Real Audience is even clearer. It can be read: "...It is the case that in a small town, called *Jeria*, and it is very certain, the earth tosses so bad smell in some areas that the animals and the birds fall dead. Going eleven cattles by this place, all eleven died. The same thing has happened to others of the same species, with donkeys, dogs, cats and hens...»

Starting from February 3rd 1731 the activity increases: "...February 3rd a new cone rose. The village of Rodeo was burned. Continuing running up to February 28th.The lava arrived to the beach after having crossed the whole surrounds district...», «...On March 7th, other cones rose and the lava went toward North, to the sea, arriving in Tingafa which was totally desolated...». Later on it continues: "...April 6th the volcano restarted with more violence and already threw an incandescent current that extended sidelong on the side of Yaiza, on the field of already formed lava...», «...On April 13th, two mountains collapsed with an awful noise and on first of May this volcanic fire was extinguished, but it was renewed 2 league farther on May 2nd, getting up new hills, coming a current of lava to threaten the place of Yaiza...».

Two new episodes, corresponding to the eruption of Mountains of *El Señalo* are clearly suitable in the newspaper: "...on June 4th, three mouths opened up at the same time. A phenomenon accompanied by violent shakes and flames appear with an awful noise. This came to sink again in the consternation to the inhabitants of the island. This new eruption was verified again near Timanfaya. The several holes met very soon only in a very high cone, from where the lava came out toward the sea...». Finally: "...on May 18th, a new cone rose in these which already rose in the same place which the ruins of Mazo, Sta. Catalina and Timanfaya are located. An open crater on the flank of this cone, rushed ashy and lightnings...».

Starting from here, the story of the priest from Yaiza becomes more concise and with less precision: "...toward the end of June 1731, the beaches and sea banks, from the West side, were covered with an incredible quantity of dead fish of all kinds of species. Toward NW, a great mass of smoke and flames, accompanied by violent detonations rose from the womb of the sea. All were seen from Yaiza. And the same thing was observed in the entire sea from the side of the Rubicón, in the western coast...».

The Priest's story finishes saying: "...in October and November (1731) new eruptions came to remove the anguishes of the island inhabitants. On December 25th 1731, the island was shaken by the most violent earth tremor that has felt in the last two disastrous years. And on December 28th, a flow of lava came out from a cone and went to Jarretas. It set on fire the place and destroyed the chapel of Saint Juan Bautista, near Yaiza...». The desperated inhabitants from Yaiza abandoned the island with the Priest, to take refuge in Gran Canaria island.

In 1733, Bishop Dávila visits the area of Yaiza and he tells us: "...This place on the foot of the volcano was not discovered in three days. When I was there, a light was only sighted, as a candle, and I stayed no more time since the powder of the sands injured my chest...»

The eruptions continue up to April 16th 1736 leaving the island desolated. The lost goods were considerable. It razed more than 200 Km². disappearing houses, country properties, plains and numerous animals. But it also caused benefits in a very certain area as in *La Geria*. The peasants of Yaiza and Tinajo discovered that the plants on the brasier charcoal took root in the earth, staying leafier and greenner. The hole also protected them from the wind. In that moment the *gerias* was built and vineyards were planted in them. But the natural misfortunes don't finish here.

The drought from 1766 to 1771 caused the third part of the population, some 2.600 people, todie from hunger and thirst.

The economic independence of the island will make possible the economic revitalization at the end of the s. XVIII. This economic independence force the island to stay in contact with foreing elemens. The new ideas arrived here from Europe. A new social conscience is been creating, not only restricted to the prevailing aristocratic environment, but to a much wider and more venturesome class: New ideas on the trade and the industry, new forms of understanding the commercial relationships, new concepts on progress. Through them, agricultural, industrial and commercial topics began to be developed.

The first half of the XIX century, several famine stages and epidemic buds started again, as the yellow fever in the years 1810 and 1811, or the flu and the pock in the years 1820 and 1825, respectively.

The catastrophes originated by new eruptions of 1824 (covered the area of *El Jable del Tao*, toward San Bartolomé and Famara) are added to this painful situation. The consequences were not as spectacular as those of Timanfaya and they were related as follows: "...In July 1824 some people began to say that they started feeling new earth trembling...", "...In the morning on the 18th in the same month, the people felt with terror the violent eruption of a volcano in Tao ... a crack appeared ... At the beginning the direction of the volcano was toward North and the eruption of materials and water continued for more than 18 hours...»

«... the lava extended throughout the places...».

On September 29th another mouth opened up, on the volcano from 1730, a league from Yaiza, going the lava toward the sea. «...Two hell mouths were formed... the noise was so much that there were nights that we couldn't fall asleep. The atmosphere was loaded so much that we hardly breathed more than sulphur. The sand rained in the whole island, and here in the roofs we could catch it with shovels... after the volcano ceased for a period of twelve days another furious eruption was presented again at six thirty in the afternoon on October 16th, 20 hours only were this last crater hurtling. Then, a column of water of something of 30 perpendicular sticks sprouted (about 30 m.)...», «...The lava ran like hot water...» «...those shower of water can be seen elevated as in cone form, and whose color is gray as ash. And they are like this way with the white of the smoke, so that the shades are sighted until one and a half or two league far...». This events ceased on October 23rd. It revived some hours later and it ended up, finally, on the 24th of the same month. «...on the 24th, the water ceased and the smoke diminished, lucky because from the mountain anything but smoke comes out...» The material damages were not considerable.

Today, the affected area by these volcanoes from 1824 is covered up the biggest part by the *jable*.

Between 1831 and 1836, as well as in 1838, another crisis was created also because of lack of rains and it was solved in 1840 with the foundation of a commission to obtain charities to remedy the misery. The situation didn't vary a lot or it was increased more until 1847 when the drought finished.

Also in this century the droughts had been occurred. The lack of liquids has been the background of the reality of Lanzarote.

The storms are less frequent, the one more remembered is the flood of 1935, by rain cause.

The emigration represented, up to the beginning of the XX century, the escape valve to the conflicting situations. The first ones took place toward Las Palmas and Tenerife, and later on, toward the American Continent -Argentina, Paraguay, Venezuela, Cuba and Mexico-.

Soon after the conference of Berlin 1.884, a new international allotment settles down due to the conflict among the European powers to get new markets. Europe distributed the African continent, as U.S.A. did with the American continent. Then the Archipelago acquired a very important international position. The same thing will happen in the First World War, in which the waters of the Archipelago will be blockade scenario and of submarine war among Englishmen and German.

At political level and from the end of the XIX century, the Canary Liberal Party, under leadership of the founder, Fernando León and Castillo, holds the absolute control. Nevertheless, at the beginning of the

«... suddenly everything calmed down and the explosion seemed to have ceased completely...».

«... it runs like honey...».

new decade, the political situation will begin to take new directions with the birth of the Canary Union Labour in 1900, beginning of what later would be the Labour Federations. Also unions or federations of republican character will be born. And, between 1917 and 1919, the Spanish Worker Socialist Party and the General Union of Workers, enter to be part of the political situation of the Archipelago.

A period of intense political life will come with the end of the dictatorship of the General Primo of Rivera that would crawl in his fall to Alfonso XIII Monarchy, and the arrival of the Republic in 1931. All this will culminate, first with a coup d'état in 1936 and, later on, until 1976, with the General Franco's dictatorship.

Socio-political Organization. On

August 16th 1982, a Statute of Autonomy was established for the Canary Islands. The constitutional law was passed by the *Cortes Generales* (Spanish Parliament) and ratified by the current King of Spain, Juan Carlos I.

According to this law, and as an expression of its own identity, the Canary Islands acceded to self government within the framework of Spanish national unity. From that time forward, the Autonomous Community assumed responsibility for the islands interests, the stable development, and the unit among all the constituents of the population.

The Canary Islands include the territories of seven islands: El Hierro, Fuerteventura, Gran Canaria, La Gomera, Lanzarote, La Palma, and Tenerife, as well as the smaller islands of Alegranza, La Graciosa, Roque del Este and Roque del Oeste, Montaña Clara and Lobos. They are under the administrative control of Lanzarote, with the exception of the last, which pertains to Fuerteventura.

The seat of the capital is shared between Santa Cruz de Tenerife and Las Palmas de Gran Canaria.

The parliament is made up by local representatives elected by universal suffrage, direct, equal, free and secret ballot.

The Canary Islands' flag features three vertical bands equal in width, whose colours, from the flagpole outwards, are white, blue, and yellow. There is also a coat of arms.

Each island, in turn, sets out the territorial organisation in township, whose local governing bodies are, respectively, the Island Councils and Municipal Councils. The Island Council (in spanish called *Cabildo*) is the body of government. The Canary government is responsible for co-ordinating the activities of the Island Councils. The Municipal Councils are the local governing body for each township.

Lanzarote is comprised of seven township: Arrecife (the island capital), Haría, Teguise, San Bartolomé, Tías, Tinajo and Yaiza.

Economy. Before the conquest, Lanzarote economy was mainly based on agriculture and livestock, as well as the recollection of wild plants species, fishing and seashell-fishing. The cultivated products were barley, called *tamoyen*, as well as corn and broad bean. Regarding livestock, goats, sheeps and pigs, were the main species. The fishing and shellfish activities, on the other hand, are likely better documented, as it is proven with the importance of *concheros* (shellfishing men) from *Fiquinineo* and *Zonzamas*. Different kind of bur varieties are outstanding among them.

Right after the conquest, and within different stages, the inhabitants from the island were dedicated to a specific dominant farming. This brings money, technical manpower and transportation, centralising about an important device to progress the island economy. These cycles are easy to detect since a model is followed with phases well delimited; fruit acclimatisation, farming consolidation, climax, slant for displacement in the outer markets and economic break down.

Chronologically, the dominant farming or the exportation has followed this order:

XVI century: archill
XVII century: vine.
XVIII century: barrilla.
XIX century: cochinilla.
XX century: onions.

The archill is a species of lichens from the rochelaceas' family, which grows on the north side of volcanic rocks, sopping up the needed humidity for its development, carried by the ocean breezes. It has a round and elongated shape (5 to 10 cm.), of gray-white

Orchilla (Archil).

Barrilla (Saltwort).

colour. It was collected and exported for using in the manufacture of dyes.

The vine was cultivated, mainly in *La Geria*, on natural, and some time artificial, *enarenados* (sand-back). The first vines were brought from the western Mediterranean area. Its surviving is an heredity of its magnificence from the past.

The grape varieties, frequently, appeared mixed within a specific area, and even within a specific exploitation. The vine production and profit is under climatic incidences since the weather of "east" or "south weather" can damage the harvest. At the same time, the raining shortage provokes the vine from growing, and producing an exceeded accumulation of sugar that turns into a raise of wine graduation. The graduation surfeit means another risk, producing illness and plague.

The *malvasía* (an elaborated wine with very sweet and aromatic grapes with big and oval grains) has been always the popular wine in the market.

By the years of 1785 and 1786, according to Alvarez Rixo, the *barrilla* started been structured, although the person who introduced the seed is unknown.

The *barrilla* is a species of plant which was collected and left to dry before being burned, and thereby converted into compact black lumps: the so-called "*barrilla* stone" . In this state it was exported to England and used as a source of soda for making soap. In the year of 1810 this growing started falling off.

The *cochinilla* (Dactylocus cocus), commonly known as *grana*, is a parasite insect that lives on the leaves of the prickly pear-cactus. The *cochinilla* growing is done on the scoop of the prickly pear-cactus, as follows: the parasite is placed in some sort of small pouch on the penca waiting to spawn. This process is initiated at the beginning of spring time. The harvest takes place during summer until autumn. Once harvested the cochineal is placed to be dried off and sieved afterwards. They are collected using a special scoop with a long stub and a bowl, a difficult and painstaking task. From the *cochinilla*, a valuable carmine day was extracted, used in making lipstick and in the colouring of fabrics.

The *cochinilla* was introduced from México as an experiment in 1826 by a Royal Order and a *Cochinilla* Acclimatisation Centre was created to teach people this new farming. Due to the subsidy given to farmers,

Vine in a hole left by the lava.

Cochinilla (Cochineal).

Watermelons on sand-bank protected by cereal.

At present, onions and vine are the main growing. The onion growing takes place in natural as in artificial sand-bank.

The sweet potato is another abundant crop. It is a tropical plant originated from America. It was introduced to farming in the *El Jable* area at the end of XIX century.

Tomato, garlic, watermelon, and melon are produced in abundance as well.

Beside the export agriculture, another agriculture of subsistence exists and within an inside-Island market (the cereals); and another only for self consuming (beans, vegetable, turnip, and fruits).

The main function of barley, the corn and even the *millo* (American corn imported by the conquers) was and still is, to become milled and toasted flour: called *gofio*.

Another important aspect for the economy are the camels (dromedary), because of the drought and misery resistance. The main productivity was for agriculture, transport and actually, the tourism.

Today, approximately 420 camels continue to exist; much less than it used to. Camel is an animal introduced from the Sahara by middle of the XIV century and its life span last between 20 to 30 years.

Fishing was also an important economic factor, what made the salt flats appear. Due to an

the production was increased. This situation, adding up the welcome of it in the international markets and the consecutive price increase, culminated around 1851-52.

The quick growth, beside the new discovery in 1862 of the aniline, a new dye, caused the price to decrease.

The villages of Guatiza and Mala are the last growing remain places where we can see how the ecological products without preservatives nor artificial additives are becoming updated in Europe after many ups and downs,.

Salt flats of Los Agujeros in the coast of Guatiza.

environmental impact and the actual economic repercussion, the fishing section is been treated as a separate section.

The salt, due to its wide purposes, has been the source for the *conejera* economy. 24 salt marshes are located in Lanzarote, but at present only two work: *Janubio* salt flats in Yaiza and *Los Agujeros* salt flats in Guatiza.

Already in the contemporaneous time, the Canary Archipelago started seeing the first economic possibilities related to tourism due to the information (brought around the world by the travelers, scientists and foreigner merchants) about the climatic conditions and benefit on some bronco-lung related illnesses.

Although as incipient, associations, clubs and sport-touristic type of organisations as *Real Club Tinerfeño, Sociedad de Fomento de Gran Canaria*, etc. were created in the period of 1900-1914. But without doubt, the decisive time and the great tourist set off should be happened from the sixty.

Although with ups and downs, the main characteristic and the grater source of income for Lanzarote is what it been converted, between 1960 and 1982, in a place for visitors all over the world.

Customs

Customs. It was transmitted most of the time by chroniclers who achieved the conquest. The aboriginal folk stories, carried on to the present, with reference to ancient beliefs, myths, and customs. At present it is difficult to know where finishing the myth and start the reality.

Still today, the marriage is contemplated in accordance with the old customs. The pregnant women, if they are on risk, drink lavender water to prevent miscarriage. Between birth and baptism, a candle is lit every night, and the old "nursery rhymes" are still remembered.

In Lanzarote, when people gather together to celebrate a familiar event, they perform some agricultural task. Also during the big festivals, they were in the habit of reciting romances, recalling legends and telling riddles more or less cunning ones. Nevertheless the "*cantares de puntas y porfias*", a kind of verbal provocation among the people, took root the most within the population. The subjects were many and variety, but were characterised by the wit, craftiness, humour and in a tearing rush thus they were improvised and answered. Sometimes the people put too much emphasis ending it up in fighting, not verbal fighting though.

We can figure out the thinking manner through these oral literature artwork, transmitted through father to sons, grandfather to grandson: regarding love and the established behaviour between man and woman; about live and death; about great natural catastrophe lived; about the emigration (to another island or country); about religion and anti-clericarism (proper from rural communities); about the ocean always present; about the countryside; about the droughts; the livestock; about the life cycle and the pass of time in the human being; about the influence of the *guanches* historical characters and their heroic deed facing the conquers, the moorish pirates; etc. Poets and philosophers have left numerous testimonies of the Canary's importance from other times. They were related with the Atlantis myth by Platón. With the end of the navigable waters by Herodoto, and with the paradise lost by Homero and Camoes... Later on *guanche* legends arose as Afche and Queen Ico. True songs of geste from a town that was threatened the freedom and the culture before the arrival of foreigners; legends related with the Moorish pirates and their incursions in the island; legends on the chiefs of Lanzarote, coloured by a legendary mist. They bring near us to the initial period of the conquest and the peninsular influence that it finished abruptly with the aboriginal time; legends of Saint Marcial; the events of the volcanic eruptions of 1730-36, and the paper that the Dolores's Virgin had in her detention. We also know the legend of the Oracle of *Vallito Negro*, place where people meet to request sinister advice to the devil; etc...

The *cabañuelas*, or prophecies, and the predictions try to guess the future in function of daily signs. They either arise from the intimate contact among the man and his physical, animal or plant environment. They are based on the observation of the rain, the evenings, the tides, the forms or formations of clouds, the direction of the wind, the attitude of the animals, the excrement of the goats, or the hair of the female camel. Signs that still maintain attentive to the oldest inhabitants in the island. The necessity to predict the weather is important since it affects to the economic activity. Some of the most popular examples are:

«If there are clouds in *Chinia*, winter will happen on the following day; Clouds in *Tremesana*, winter in a week».

« If the North weather is good weather. If the *majorero* (from Fuerteventura) weather brings rains; the Africa weather is drying and bad, it leaves people intimidated; the time of breeze is when the wind blows in La Graciosa».

«If the horizons on Saint Mateo day (September 21st) dawn clear, good year; if they are foggy, bad one».

«If the excrement of the goats comes undone easily in autumn, good year.»

« Everybody went to see the tide early to the beach, at five in the morning, in Saint Juan day (June

24th). If the tide dawns ascending, good presage; full, at the maximum level, excellent year; if it dawns lowering, bad one».

Out of all animals, the goat is the one that mostly is observed to deduce from its behaviour.

«The goats fight when supposing wind. If they have an inflated mouth, the weather is going to be bad».

Also fanaticism, superstitions, and witches are present, for which the power of the Saints are invoked to in exchange for promises or wearing of amulets. The most average superstitions are those that carry the misfortune or the death, although there are other more benign ones.

«It is sinned to kill *pispas* (lapwing), the little bird of Saint María, because when the Virgin escaped with her Son to Egypt they erased the prints left by their feet so that the Jews wouldn't find them».

«The house that has an *aromero* (acacia) it will be unfortunate».

«The presence of quails in the field are good sign».

«The appearance of the hoopoes in the fields are signs of good crop and happiness».

«The white spots in the fingernails indicate that the person is a liar».

«To the ones that have warts it is because they spend time in counting the stars at night».

The promises consist on offerings candles or wax figure. In some hermitages wax hands, arms, heads or animals can still be seen. In general, women make this type of promises.

People make to Saint Roque promises so that they don't come up with contagious illnesses; to Saint Isidro so that the fields prosper; to Saint Andrés to make rain. People who suffer from the eyes appeal to Saint Lucía. The navigators to the Virgen del Buen Viaje (Virgin of the good trip); and this way with a score of Saints.

Amulets used to be and still are all type of medals with Saints and Virgins, scapulars, or pieces of the Gospels.

The popular medicine also counts with remedies for the common illnesses and it is with the help of sangrias in the arms, infusions, frictions with mixtures, water of herbs and plants, enemas and purges, cataplasms and other "stews" that are able to cure the

Painting with lime: "encalado" (whitewashing).

pneumonia; the palsy or muscular weakness; the *romadizo* or nose cold; the diarrhea; the eye bad luck; the headache; the burns; and a long etc... of illnesses. Special mention to the *cucas* (cockroaches) tripes to eradicate the toothache. As according to the tradition, when the pain persists it is attributed to the aching "patient" didn't want to take the prescribed *cucas* tripes.

In September, who has bread would sow. Or «no camel can see his córcova (hump)». We finish this section with these two good porverbs of popular customs. Although we will leave you in suspense with the answer of the following riddle:

« He walks and doesn't have feet,
He eats and doesn't have mouth
and he finds little
all the food.» ...   What is it?

Fiestas (Festivities). At present, the *fiestas* are related more or less to the old culture. Each town celebrates an annually *fiesta* to the Saint. Each temple was built by the people economic effort.

The popular *fiestas* constitute one of the scarce festival events in the island. Participation, spontaneity, generosity, and the simplicity of elements are their main components. New clothes are bought, the facades are whitewashed. People decorate the doors, the squares are decked out with bouquets and flags. Heads are killed, *verbenas* are mounted. They make sweets, common foods, blazes, and people go to the beach to enjoy. They are the suitable dates so that the *parrandas* (sprees) interpret the most traditional airs in our folklore (*isas, folías, seguidillas* or *malagueñas*).

The most important popular *fiestas,* with religious character, are devoted to the patron of Lanzarote: Saint Marcial, in Femés (Yaiza) on July 7th. It is the first religious image that was brought to the island; and the Virgin of Los Dolores or Los Volcanes, in Mancha Blanca (Tinajo), on September 15th, and as vocation sign when saving the population from the volcanic catastrophe of 1730-36.

The *Ranchos de Ánimas* (Ranches of Souls) were formed in November, month of the Deceased and new wine. Groupings that got funds for the deceased masses in cheerful parties which hid the sadness for the memory of the dear beings. Habit is already almost out-of-date.

On December 13th, day of Saint Lucía, "games of *La Santa*" were carried out. Word games that were penalized with garments. It was an important *Fiesta* in Yaiza and Tinajo. Unfortunately these word games are almost lost. At the present time with the purpose of recovering them, is summoned their celebration openly in Tías,.

Christmas dates are other moments in which numerous and important folkloric manifestations can be shared. People have the habit of reproducing the scene of Christ's Birth; to sing carols -that have suffered adaptations to the melodies of the *isas* and *folías* -; and to form the Ranches of Easter, mainly in Teguise and San Bartolomé. The Ranches of Easter are a derivation of the old Ranches of Souls that have lost the collector character and they go out only in December to sing allusive Christmas verses.

In Femés, with their tradition to the shepherding, «inns» were common. The shepherds went from house to house requesting inn for Joseph and Mary. Another particularity of Femés was the *Hogueras* (campfire). A black dressed puppet with buck horns, camel excrements, donkey and a lot of salt (Evil symbol) are burned.

The Carnivals are organized in February. They are costume *Fiestas*; the liberation of the desires, the return to the childhood, the trip to the age, and the critic to the public characters. People group called *murgas* and satirical songs are composed to sing all together. They last three days and they conclude on Ash- Wednesday with the Sardine Funeral. The most important takes place in Arrecife and the most traditional *parranda* (to go on a spree) is *Los Buches*. Adorned with popular suits and the faces covered with nets, the streets travel singing and treating to skillful and catastrophe inoffensive blows with voluminous fish crops, previously inflated and dryings in the sun. This spree is the only contact with the old carnival of Arrecife . Their songs are a small proof of the well-of sea songs from Lanzarote. There are some of the verses here:

«The Carnivals already leave,
good thing, not very hard
and now the Lent comes
to confess with the priest.»
...
«Mulattress runs next to my bed
to calm this horrible pain
and if you hold me on to your chest
my heart won't suffer any more.»

Carnivals of Las Breñas (Yaiza) are also famous. The houses open the doors to receive people. The *mascaritas* (people with small masks) make fun and they get some thing to keep in a small basket hanging down the arm.

In June Saint Juan's typical bonfire, Saint Andrés and Saint Martín's sprees, formerly corresponded to the *fiestas* of sowing, the wine, and the livestock slaughters.

Saint Juan's festivity (June 24th) has a special acceptance and it consists of four parts: The Eve, The Dawn, The Morning and The Afternoon. In the Eve, the gorse strokes were brought to light and to feed the blazes. *Millo* pineapples and sweet potatoes were roasted. People drank wine and the blazes were jumped. They got ready the loving *agüeros* (omens that the marriageable women carried out to guess the name, the social position, the profession of the future husband). At Dawn medicinal plants were picked up, cures, predictions, and some "cleanings" in the houses were made with water of flowers. They were also proven the omens prepared the previous night. The Morning was the moment to attend the religious ceremonies. And The Afternoon was the time of the sea baths, beginning this way the advisable season of baths. These immersions with doctor-preventive purposes, including also animals, are believed that came from the *guanche* time The day concluded with dances in the town of Soo, in Teguise whose patron is Saint Juan.

Other *fiestas* to highlight are: the descent of the Virgin of Las Nieves, in Teguise, on August 5th. Saint Roque, in Tinajo on August 16[th.] And the Virgin of Los Remedios, in Yaiza, on September 8th.

Almost all the remaining patron fiestas of the island are carried out during summer time, coinciding with the months of smaller activity in the traditional agricultural works.

The *fiestas* and the rest of the cultural practices are affected for a process of cultural criterion as consequence of the society modernization. The unitary, collective and intimate character from before are getting lost to open the way to people's massive entrance who spend their free time in *fiestas* of towns.

As we have said before, these *fiestas* are related intimately with the music and the traditional dances. The folklore of nowadays supposes the search and the adaptation, on the part of studious in the topic, previous and later old songs to the conquest.

Of the aboriginal music it is known very little. Instruments were very poor: rustic elements of percussion of feet and hands, sound necklaces with bead of marine snails and shells of limpets («limpet tablespoons»). Starting from the conquest new instruments were incorporated: tambourines, triangles, castanets, *raspadores de caña* (cane raspers), etc. And later on: guitars, mandolins, lutes, and *timples* . The *timple* is the most representative instrument in the folklore canary musical. Also called, *camellito* (small camel), and it consists on an adaptation of the Iberian guitar, with lengthened narrow body and convexed underneath. It can vary the number of strings and the tuning according to the island. Lastly, the *forito* or accordion is the instrument whose presence is considered indispensable.

With the new instruments new songs and dances were created:

- *Isas*: relatively recent songs (years 40-50) coming from old *conejera* musical rules. In the dance, the men execute their movements taking a stick with a traditional wool backpack in the superior end,.

- *Malagueñas*: plaintive songs that make allusion, generally, to the love for the earth or for the dead mother. It is a derivation of the Andalusian *fandango* and has as peculiarity the existence of a chanted refrain appearing after each soloist. The dance is, fundamentally, soloists. The man manages the woman, or the women, in his choreographic evolution.

- *Folías*: it is one of the dearest folkloric representations. It comes from a Baroque dance becoming popular along the XVII and XVIII centuries. It is composed of two parts of eight compasses each one repeating with variations. The dance is executed by a single person, which is accompanied of castanets.

- *Seguidillas*: as literary verse they know each other from half of the XV century and as musical manifestation from the time of the Catholic Kings. They are sung by several soloists (so many as it is possible) in a successive order.

Procession of Curpus on salt floor in the town of Tinajo.

- *Sorondongos*: originated back to an infantile game of the XVI century. The dance is carried out in men and women circles and with a person in the center that develops simple movements and taking turns.

- *Sarandas*: it is a recent creation (seventies) but it has soaked in the *conejera* tradition. The dance is developed around a *saranda* (farm tool used to move the grain) sustained on high by a group of men and women in alternate order and imitating the movements carried out in the field.

Besides the patron *fiestas*, the social frame more used for the folkloric expressions were *bailes de candil* (lamp dances). Lively dances taken place in small living rooms illuminated by a lamp of petroleum, carbide or oil and livened up by small sprees. A variant of these were "Saint Pascual's dances», in honor to Saint Pascual Bailón. A candle was placed with a knot in between. In the first place the men took out to dance the women and when the candle arrived to the knot, the women chose couple. When the room was very small, the men paid a *taifa* to dance, then they were known as «*taifas* dance». In Lanzarote they were also called "governors' dance", because a person (called the governor) with a stick was placed to control and to avoid the fights among men. In some moment of the dance the music was stopped and they organized songs of challenges and insistences between men and women, or among them alone.

Starting from the forties this type of dances began to disappear.

It is necessary to thank the survival on behalf of the folklore to the *Agrupación Ajey*, been founded in 1940, and later on to the *Agrupación Los Campesinos* (Peasants Grouping), in 1970. Without them this section had been part of the History.

Traditional games. These playful manifestations of cultural root have stayed in the course of the time thanks to the popular participation and lately to the work of some specialists of the topic investigation.

Among the field games more significant and practised in Lanzarote we will mention the following ones: *Lucha Canaria* (Canary Wrestling), *Lucha de Garrote y Lata* (Fight with Truncheon and Can), *Lanzamiento y Esquiva de Piedras* (Stone Launching and Avoiding), *Juego del Palo* (Game with Stick), *Salto del Pastor* (Jump of the Shepherd), *Salto de la Vara* (Jump with Stick), *Vela Latina* (Latin Candle), *Barquillos* (Small boats) , *Pelotamano* (ball in hand), *Bola Canaria* (Canary Ball), *Arrastre de Ganado* (Haulage of Livestock), *Piña* (Pineapple), *Billarda* (Billiards), and *Levantamiento de Arado* (Rising of Plow).

An important group of these games was already practiced in the aboriginal culture. The economic activities have their origin and relationship with these games. In general, they are very similar games from other towns. There are other games coming from the establishment of the Europeans. Thus, the *Pelotamano* and the Games with Balls are introduced by the conquerors, with all security, at the beginning of the XV century.

The games of saloon are also broadly represented: *Seiseño, Tute, Politana, La Primera* (the First one), *El Burro* (the Donkey), *Brisca or El Truco* (Trick).

The origin of most of the board games, as well as the divinatory and hurtling type have their starting point in magic rituals. They are chance games and the decision doesn't depend on the player.

In most of the cases they are subject to a ritual explaining the reason of certain spaces for games, the attendance of distinguished personalities, the

Playing Skittles in the town of La Caleta de Famara.

celebration of parallel ceremonies, the rule, certain materials, etc.

The traditional games and sports reflect, also, the values of the town. These evolve in the measure as they are part of the culture, although many stay through the time. They are also good to demonstrate who the best is and therefore it is an important mechanism of reaching prestige. Challenge and bets are associated, for what some have reached, lately, certain level of economic competitiveness. Such it is the case of the *Lucha Canaria* (Canary Wrestling) taken to some fighters to a considerable social improvement.

At the present time, the traditional games are in fashion after persisting for not disappearing. For that reason it is easy to see some of these games in the towns of Lanzarote; in their gathering and their *fiestas*. The most practiced is the Game of the Skittles.

Long life to the traditional games !.

Arts and Crafts.
In Lanzarote, as in so many old towns, the ceramic was part of the daily life of the old inhabitants. The vessels were used for food preparation or for storage and food transportation, as Abreu Galindo points out: «...they ate in *gánicos* of mud cooked in the sun, as big pans...».

Making palm hats.

As in the rest of the Archipelago, before the lathe potter's discovery, the Lanzarote ceramic was handmade and it was of low quality. They carried out their kitchen furniture and pots superimposing to a base of mud -that sometimes mixed with other clays, small stones or marine shells- a series of cylinders until arriving to the desired height. Later on, they were planed to give them bigger consistency before the definitive cooking. The decoration was made by incision and it was quite simple, with the help of parallel, horizontal, vertical lines, triangles, and broken lines.

Besides the ceramic there are other handmade techniques for stone, wood, brass, palm, wicker, cane, rush, using old technique. These have left transmitting from generation to generation, what represents one of the cultural relics of this island.

The handmade activities are distributed by the whole island and there are stores of craft in different municipalities. Although most of the stores are in Arrecife and the tourist centers. For the one that wants to observe how they are carried out the different works they can go to the shops. We will give a general relationship of the different points and the different activities. For the exact address it is better to ask inside the town.

For works in stone (stonemason, piles of distilling water or figured stones), there are shops in Haría, Teguise and San Bartolomé.

For works with wood (useful for farm, *timples* of pumpkins or barrels), you can go to Haría, Teguise, San Bartolomé, La Vegueta, Yaiza and Playa Blanca.

There are only two tinman in the entire island, one in Teguise and the other in Arrecife.

For works in palm, wicker, cane, rush or whistling (baskets, brooms, mats, dolls, hats,...) you can find them in Máguez, Haría, Punta Mujeres, Los Valles, Teguise, Tinajo, Monument to the Peasant, San Bartolomé, Arrecife, La Asomada, Mácher and Yaiza.

For the making of fabrics (bobbins, embroideries, soaked, crochet hook, spun, *macramé* or looms) there are shops in Máguez, Haría, Punta Mujeres, Los Valles, Teguise, Tinajo, Monument to the Peasant, San Bartolomé, Arrecife, La Asomada, Mácher and Yaiza.

And for pottery and ceramic works you can go to Haría, Teguise, Tinajo, Monument to the Peasant, Mozaga, Arrecife and Yaiza.

Every Sunday morning there is a flee market in Teguise where you can find all kinds of trinkets, besides some stands of true craft. If you can't find what you looked for, you will find a good atmosphere anyway.

ARCHITECTURE.

Ancient Architecture.

The activities of the people who have inhabited Lanzarote over the centuries have left their mark on the island's unique landscape, whose material and social manifestations constitute an important cultural patrimony. This important cultural patrimony incorporates important monuments and an infinity of insular spaces that define and summarize its former history, telling us about the style of living of its inhabitants.

The ancient architecture (according to the character of the different elements which constitute the island architectural patrimony) has been divided into four groups:

- Religious structures
- Unique structures
- Industrial archaeology structures
- Residential structures.

Religious Structures. These include nine churches, some thirty hermitages scattered throughout the island and two convents in the town of Villa de Teguise.

The churches were built as the different population centers developed, with delay to the style of its historical period.

Church of Femés.

According to their wealth, the local churches express the economic situation for which, at particular time in the history, the towns went through. The constructions of churches used to be scattered in different periods and most of them have been reconstructed for different causes, like fires, pirate incursions or to perform enlargements.

Each one features singular characteristics, such as, the church of the Virgin Nuestra Señora de los Remedios from the town of Yaiza, built on an irregular geometrical construction site. Or the small church of Saint Marcial in the town of Femés, with its arcade and chafts of columns decorated with unique collarets. Or the Parish Church of Teguise, the oldest of the island (1440-45). Through several plunders and vandalism, new chapels were added to it by some families who had the right to be buried there. Later on, in 1727, the bell tower was built with an octagonal edge end covered by wood.

Most of the hermitages were built during the XVIII century. Erected by the neighbours themselves, therefore, they are remarkable for the simplicity of construction and material used.

The hermitage used to be constructed with a rectangular body, with a sacristy room attached alongside. Volcanic stone ashlaring appear at the corners of some of these hermitages. The ceilings, with two slopes, used to be made of wood and covered with flat moulded *adobe* (sun-dried brick), and in some cases, festooned with a roofing tile line. In the hermitage austere interiors, there used to be a small pulpit, a baptismal font, an altar-peace, and some paintings with religious portrayals.

The purpose of the hermitage constructions was due to appearances most of the time, such as the Nuestra Señora de las Nieves appeared to a small shepherd. The hermitage of the Virgin Nuestra Señora de las Nieves is recalled from the XVI century, although it is possible that it was established during the Conquest. Pilgrimages were another example for veneration of the Virgin. These have a festive atmosphere. In this hermitage, and from 1725 to the middle of the present century, the descent of the Virgin of Teguise celebration takes place to promote the rain.

Regarding Saint Francisco convent only the church last. It is the ninth convent of the Franciscan Order on this island. It was initially built in 1588, about 50 m. from the Parish of Teguise. In 1618 it was fired and destroyed by the attack of pirates Xabác and Solimán, being rebuilt two years later by the believers' contributions. In 1835 the convent was definitively passed by the civil control. At present the convent, after it was restored,has been rehabilitated for cultural purposes.

The other convent, Saint Domingo, was founded in 1698 by the captain Rodríguez Carrasco for the Domi-

Hermitage of Máguez.

nica Order. After suffering many artistic crashes, this convent constitute today the architectonic collective of the *Ayuntamiento* (City Hall) and the church of Saint Domingo. The convent's facade, with double composition, presents a lateral reed-mace to the left, two big doors, and a glazed circular hole. A symbol of the Dominica Order is found above the right door with red profile.

Unique Structures. This category includes buildings which, for their location, use or origin are considered unique: cemeteries, forts, lighthouses and warehouses (*Cillas, Taros* and *Maretas*).

Until the beginning of the XIX century, the deceased were buried beneath the floor of the churches, hermitages, or in the summits of the mountains, maybe before the supposed belief that there it was nearer the cosmos. From that time forward, the first cemeteries were built, today totalling ten and excluding the most recent ones, the other ones respond to the traditional aesthetics: walls of stone and lime with small pyramidal endings, rectangular bases, and the chapel to the rear.

The fortifications arise for the necessity of defending the island and for that purpose four castles were built: the castle of *Las Coloradas* or Tower of *El Aguila* in the south coast; the castle of Saint Gabriel and Saint José, in Arrecife; and the castle of Saint Bárbara, in Teguise.

The castle of *Las Coloradas* (1741) has a round floor base and with trunk-conical shape with two-story structures: with barrel vault in the upper level which sustained the *aljibe* (reservoir). The lower levels contained living quarters and service rooms. Both the upper and lower levels contained an air ditch which is insulated from the outside.

Saint Gabriel castle (1573) has a square plan with four ramparts in diamond shape and a wooden interior distribution.

Castle of Las Coloradas or Tower of the Aguila.

Front door of the parochial church of Teguise.

Cilla (church warehouse) of Teguise.

Saint Bárbara castle (1588) has a rhomboidal plan, with strong lay brick walls and circular towers.

And finally, Saint José castle (1779) has a semicircular plan with two superimposed hares, a barrel vault, a gunpowder tank, dungeons, and a reservoir.

In the sections of the municipalities we will give more data of these constructions that nowadays, once reconstructed, they have cultural utility.

The six lighthouses are not very important for highlighting their architectural qualities. There are four in Arrecife: *Mármoles* lighthouse, *Vareadero*, *Puerto*

Naos, and *Muelle Chico*. There is one in *Punta Fariones*, and another in *Punta Pechiguera* with square plan, central patio,and a tower attached on the side. The latest is in very bad condition but it has an attached of modern construction .

As for the traditional systems of storage three types can be distinguished : *Cillas, Taros*, and *Maretas*.

The *Cillas* are warehouses that were built by the church to store products obtained through tithes and its own harvests. The most important is the *Cilla* of Teguise from the first half of the XVIII century. This

Cemetery of Yaiza.

Mareta (Surge) in the fields of Guatiza.

warehouse is located in the main square of Teguise and it is a construction of rectangular plant with thick stone and earthen walls. The cover has double roof with two slopes kept in a good condition.

The *Taros* are rural structures pertaining to the architectural tradition of the local agrarian economy, which served as the functions of *silo*, dairy and storage facility for farm utensils. They usually have a circular base, three to five meters in diameter, and three to six meters high, depending on whether they are one or two story levels. They were constructed using stone, loam and lime. At present none is conserved worthy of pointing out.

The *Maretas* are deposits of water for agriculture and for personal consumption. They are usually located in the slopes of mountains or they are connected by channels. Some can still be seen by the fields, mainly in the area of Guatiza-Mala, although they are no longer used for this purpose. They have a circular or rectangular shape and half-buried. They are built with stone and lime. The roof as a vault made of stone. The central deposit, called *caidera* receives the water from the strainer. The construction of this most important type in the island was the *Gran Mareta*, deposit of water in *Gran Aldea* (town aborigine located in the current Teguise), located in the skirt of the mountain *Guanapay*. It had 40 meter of diameter and 9.2 meter of depth. In 1560, The *Gran Mareta*, appears as a good for the treasury for what all the people of the island have right to their waters. It was destroyed in 1975 for housing construction purposes.

Archaeological Industrial Structures. This designation is given to buildings that belonged to the island economy: Tanneries, *Tahonas* (Crushing Mills), Mills, Lime Ovens, and Salt-flats.

The Tanneries include the structures and tanks required for the various processes involved in the tanning of leathers. Today there are not any worthy of pointing out.

The machines of milling grain have a vital importance since the island main activity is based on cereal and cattle farm type.

It starts with the hand mill, of Roman origin, simple in its use and with materials easy to get and to work. They are formed by two pieces, called molars, circular and the same size leaning on one another. It also has a long stick finished in tip to be introduced in a series of unperfored holes located in the upper stone, serving as support in the movement. The material of these stones *"piedras molineras"* is basalt. They are of family character and had frequent use in the houses to mill the *gofio* that was consumed on a daily basis.

From these mills were derived the *tahonas* that have a community character. We know about them since beginning of the XVIII century. It was worked by a group of people (*"moliendo a bote"* = "milling like boat") or, generally, by a camel that was hooked to the *almijarra*, a piece that worked the complex mechanism of millstones, gutter bearings, wheelspindles, etc. Then the grain was introduced by the mill-hopper. They are usually in square haves, with stone walls, mud and lime

Tahona (Crushing-mill) of Museo al Campesino (Museum dedicated to the Peasant) in Mozaga.

Mill of Tiagua.

with roofs of one or two slopes covered by plates of mud and straw. Many *tahonas* are still preserved and one can observe its operation in *Casa Museo del Campesino* in Mozaga (Museum House of the Peasant of Mozaga).

The *tahonas* was substituted in turn by the mills and later on by the *molinas*.

The mills are machines that were used to mill grain or to bring the water up from the sea toward the *cocederos* (water heating flat) of the salt-flats. The mills appear on the island during the XVII and XVIII centuries constituting a singular element of the landscape. Popularly speaking, they are known with the name of *pajeros*.

The rubble-work structure has three storey levels. The stocks of the mill (canvases, tools, spare parts, etc...) are located in the first floor. The *gofio* is picked up and the sacks are placed on the second floor in a handy place. And finally the operation machinery is located on the third floor. Over there, the grain is lifted up to introduce it through the mill-hopper, going to the second floor already milled. They have a circular plan with tronco-cónical section and finished off by a wooden plate "hut", from where the sweeps come

Molina (mill) de Teguise.

through. It is mounted on a double wooden ring that is guided by means of an axis or helm according to the direction of the wind . The machinery has a grind-stone where the spindle is left up, and it ends up in a lantern. This lantern gears with the jagged wheel fixed to the semi-horizontal axis of the crosses. They are usually, wooden of firebrand, being supplemented with white stick, chestnut tree and fig.

The *molinas*, of more modern type (XIX century), establish an accused difference between the machinery and the construction. They are mills with four to six sails and with horizontal axis. They lean on wooden bearings distributing the movement by means of the "wheel" to a metallic screw. The vertical offspring moves the two stones located in the lower part of the triangular wooden structure. The whole group of the structure leans on in its inferior axis. It is able to move by means of a wooden stick in order to guiding it to the dominant winds. The construction of stone factory and local pargeting factory (with square plan) have a single long-side for the mill and warehouse . Some have annexed rooms for housing.

With the disappearance of the agriculture of the cereal as source of subsistence these machines of the human invention are mainly today a tourist advertising.

The ovens of lime appear in the XVII century due to the exploitation of the lime. This was used to purify the rain water, to whiten and for housing construction. They are distributed according to the salpeter bed areas and to the external trade. Those with circular plan prevail on the rectangular and mixed ones. The types of materials vary as they are of coal or firewood. Those of firewood are smaller. They are usually circular, among three and six meter of diameter and with a single opening. Some are half-buried or located in the ravines to facilitate the introduction of raw material and the extraction of the elaborated product. Those of coal, with export purposes, are usually rectangular and with four to sixteen meters long, reaching up more than ten meters high, and they can have up to four openings of different sizes. The process of production of the lime has stayed unalterable in its form from the Roman time until the fifties when the cement appears. The raw material (*caliche*) for its production comes fundamentally from deposit locations formed by fossil beaches, being extracted the stone in form of chips. Once the chips are divided and their sludges eliminated, the oven can be loaded. The stones arrived until a grilled of iron leaving free the inferior section to be able to begin the combustion that was made with dry furzes. Firewood layers or vegetable coal were introduced among the stones and at the end the material cone was covered with earthen coal. The total combustion of the material column lasted among three to four days. The obtained cold lime were extinguished with salted water and it was sieved to remove the sludges.

The history of the salt is mistaken with regards to the big civilizations. The oldest reference on its social organization dates from the old China (2205-2197 b. C.). The taxes which it has always supported have been, until near dates, a source of basic resources for the different States. In spite of all the advances of the chemistry and the engineering of the cold, this universal product has demonstrated to have a capacity of survival almost magical.

Very few written references exist regarding the salt production in Canary for the old inhabitants. It is known that they obtained it directly from the puddles of the high tide and with that the fish was salted. These puddles, in some places, were manipulated for a bigger production. So we can dare seying that some built salt flat could exist before the Conquest.

After the Conquest the natural *cocederos* belong to noble property, having the vicinity the right of use. It is starting from 1525 when the Crown gives this right to private hands. And in 1605, the existent salt flat was incorporated to the monopoly of the Real Treasury. Starting from then it is when the first development takes place of salt flat in the islands. The second great salt flat appearance takes place between 1910 and 1930, especially in Lanzarote, to satisfy the demand of the canning industry.

It is in Lanzarote where the oldest salt flats are found in the Archipelago. The salt flats *El Río* on the foot of the cliffs of *Famara*, were exploited almost for sure, in Roman time although news are only found on conditioning works in the times of Sancho de Herrera, first Lord of Lanzarote, at the end of the XV century. Until the year 1775 there is not information regarding the creation of a new salt flat in the *Charco de San Ginés* (Arrecife). At the end of the XIX century those in *Puerto Naos* are developed, being these the last built salt flats with mud.

After the disappearance of the salt taxes at the beginning of this century and the application of a new technology in their construction, with stone linings and lime, they resurge again to supply, the also flourishing, industry of the salting. Until middle of the twenties, they appear then, by chronological order: *Berrugo*

Salt flats of El Janubio.

(Playa Blanca), *Janubio, La Santa,* those in *Costa Teguise, Los Charcos, Las Cucharas* and some more in *Puerto Naos.* In the forties they arise with the appearance of the salt flats of *Orzola* again, *Punta Mujeres, los Agujeros, Tío Joaquín, Rostro, Bastián, Las Caletas, Los Mármoles, La Bufona* and four more in Puerto Naos. In the sixties the last ones are built; *El Reducto* and *Guasimeta.*

The canning factory crisis and the appearance of the cold industry put an end to this industry. Nowadays only the remains last with two exception witness: *Janubio* and *Los Agujeros.*

Salt flats of El Río (the River) seen from the cliffs of Famara.

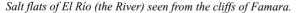

Salina of Los Agujeros (The Holes).

The salt flats of the *Janubio* are the biggest size of Canary and for their architectonical and hydraulics complexity we can say that it is one of the salt flat inventions more important of the world, thanks to Víctor Fernández, *El Salinero* (Las Breñas, 1844-1920). The sea water (4º of salt flat concentration) it is captured by receivers in the lagoon and they are risen by five seal mills and foil multiseal anchored in bases of stone of different levels (nowadays it is carried out by means of diesel moto-bombs). This water goes from the main pipe surrounding the *cocederos* to those that it feeds. The water stays in the *cocederos* for a period of 15 to 20 days, and it changes up to five transfers of recipients. The process, called *curtido* has for object to go up the salt flat concentration up to 20º. Later on it passes to the cuts, or crystallizing, through pipes. The whole group is protected by cut-wind walls of volcanic stone. In the cuts it stays about 20 days again until the total precipitation of the salt takes place. They are usually carried out between 12 and 14 "caught" a year from March to October. The salt is accumulated in the lateral banks where it allows to slip and to purge until the following one caught. The rest of the year is used for maintenance works and restoration. At the moment, and after being legally protected, they are in restoration phase. The group constitutes one of the emblematic points of Lanzarote given its historical, landscaping, architectural, etnográphic, cultural and ecological great interest.

Residential Structures. There are two general categories of residences: the traditional houses reflecting folk architecture of the island and the Seigniorial or Lordly residences.

Transfer of water from the cocederos to the well.

House in the town of Los Valles.

The rural housing are the best examples of popular architecture where the local outline, with little changes have been conserved. There are also good examples in the main urban groupings as in Arrecife and mainly in Teguise, which is almost conserved the same as when was built by the hosts of the Crown of Castile.

This popular architecture was anonymous from the beginning, adapting to these places Andalusian and Extremadura models which have been transforming according to the peculiarities of the region until reaching their own characteristic. One of these peculiarities are the African winds, which their inhabitants defend themselves with thick walls and without any opening toward the exterior.

The structure of the popular house is very simple. The ground floor has a quadrilateral form, with another central square inside, forming the patio to which the rooms open up, not communicated to each other, and were increasing according to the possibilities and necessities.

The constructive materials come from easy access places, with little or null transformation. They are found in the means or brought by the sea. Initially it was built with dry stone, then with stones agglutinated in mud, later on with lime and lately with blocks of volcanic sand and cement. The roofs have usually two slopes, initially formed by *pírganos* (central nerve of the leaf of the palm), thorns or bobos branches (glaucous Nicotiana); later on slats and teak boards were used for their interior structure. The covers are made of plates; clay mixture, and wheat straw. The external treatment of the walls is carried out "by spoon" (coating without using the trowel to flatten) being a rough surface on which the successive layers of lime are superimposed.

The housings are located, habitually, near the productive activity and they are usually oriented to-

Technology of the salt			
Harvesting	Harvest the salt deposited in a natural way: in shore-cliffs, small lagoons, coastal or big continental deposits.		
Mining Industry	Obtaining of salt by means of mining uses of salt gem		
Graduation and boiling	Obtaining of salt from heating of the sea water or the brine in recipients of different materials using some class of fuel until producing the evaporation of the water and the precipitation of the salt.		
Concentration and evaporation (it only uses solar energy)	**Extensive Saline**	The crystallization doesn't appear divided. They are usually interior, of spring.	
	Intensive Saline (all the Canary saline)	**Naturals**	High tide puddles on muddy or rocky shore-cliff lands. They only possess the still.
		Artificials (they consist of: reception and impulsion, still, watering systems and crystallization)	**Primitive on rock.** They have two recipients: the still and the crystallization vessel or surge. The reception system is by means of an overflow connected to the still. They are circular and closed with stone walls and mud or mortar of lime.
			Ancient of mud. Generally settled on accumulations of alluvial character. The walls of the still and pipes are made of stones caught with mortar of lime and waterproofed with mud or lime. The bottoms are of rammed mud. Saline of El Río.
			Ancient of mortar of lime. Masonry factory of basaltic stones caught with mortar of lime, as much the walls as the bottoms.
			New of mud with stone linings. Typical of Lanzarote. Except for those from El Río. All the other ones are of this type. The position of the still is invested. Now they are in the interior and the water moves toward the cuts closer to the coast. The cuts are composed: divided by interior "*pareditas*" (stop). They are built with stone and mud, being only used the lime for the impermeabilization inside the pipes. The bottoms are of rammed mud.

House of the Arroyo's Family in Arrecife.

ward SE. The simplest are mainly in the shepherding and fishing areas , called " *tegalas* ". they are made of dry stone with branches in the roof and they have a temporary utility.

The most important thing was the kitchen and the reservoir. Other facilities like the press, the cellar, the thrashing-floor, the number of corrals, the drying shed, the wooden type or the number of windows, gave them a more special character. The kitchen executed bedroom and meeting place functions. To cook the foods a *tenique* was used (stone in which the fire of gorses or trunks were threwn); then the *reverdero* was used (small apparatus that worked with alcohol); and later, the fuse kitchens and the bellows spirit lamps with petroleum were introduced.

The ovens are in the kitchens and when they are located inside, the body of the oven comes out. It has a cubic or cylindrical base and the superior part is finished off by a spherical cap. The interior of this cap is hollow and covered by a special, slight and volcanic stone that maintains the heat.

The chimneys forms the finishing off of the kitchens, with different shapes and some of them with obvious Moorish influences.

The reservoirs were built on a slight decline of the land. The water, in its track, went by the strainer (a structure with a filter of blackish gorses) that serves as retaining the sediments. When the water of the reservoir was drained, the well was used.

The lordy housing, with Portuguese, Andalusian and Castilian colonial influences, is bound to the lord, ecclesiastical, administrative or military power. Good examples, well conserved are: Arroyos' house and the houses of Fajardo street in Arrecife; Curbelo House in Arrieta; House of the gentlemen Paz Currás and Antonio López Socas in Haría; the house of the Mayor Guerra and house of Ajei in San Bartolomé; the housing of Clemente Perza in Los Valles; Espínola house, Diezmos house, Parish house and house of Marqués Agustín of Herrera y Rojas, among other, in Teguise.

Contemporary architecture. We

have to differ among the residential architecture, (clearly marked for their parallelism), the traditional popular housing; the monumental architecture; and big hotels and tourist centers.

To be about this topic it is unaboidable to come closer to César Manrique's figure. This symbolic person from Lanzarote, introduced basic concepts of ecology, popular architecture, preservation, and adaptation of the landscape to the tourist necessities. With his work has impeded the development of an indiscriminate tourism and far from the roots and natural environments so frequent in other places. He was able to convince as much to the politicians as to the inhabitants of the island to follow some common guidelines. To such an extent that he became the ideologist of Lanzarote as well as for other countries. He has been able to balance the natural with that created by the man and to establish a harmony between the traditional and the most avant-garde signs. Volcanic materials, forms, spaces, traditional constructions and vegetation; scum and misery for some, they have ended up being, once gone by his hands, the authentic signs of identity of a modern culture. So much the architectural development as tourist of this island in the last twenty years goes together to César Manrique's life, for what reviewing his biography we can study this evolution.

César Manrique. He was born in Arrecife, in April 24th, 1919. He studied in the Superior School of Fine Arts of Madrid where he could be impregnated of the surrealist currents of the fifties. From this time, years 50 and 53 respectively, his first important works are related with Lanzarote: the murals of the *Parador* (Inn) of Tourism of Arrecife and those of the lobby of Guasimeta airport. In the year 1955 he obtains the second medal of the I Excibition of Contemporary Art of

César Manrique Foundation.

Cartagena. He participates in the XXVIII Biennial of Venice and in the III Hispanic-American Biennial taken place in La Havana.

Thanks to José Ramírez -the other great exciting and designer of the *Futuro Lanzarote* (Lanzarote Future)- César Manrique never lose his contact with the island. Although he travelled and exposed all over the world. In 1965 he decided to settle in New York. Then he returned in 1968 to be devoted entirely, together with his friend and President of the Insular Town Council, José Ramírez, in an artistic project on Lanzarote. In this year the *Jameos del Agua* was adapted for the tourism on his idea, and he designed the Fecundity sculpture, built in honor to the rural *conejero.*

In the same year his house was built in *Taro* of Tahiche. The building is located on five volcanic bubbles of a colada from the 1730 eruption. It has two storeys. Inspired by the traditional architectureon, he added elements like big windows on the lava, functional transparent spaces, and wide terraces on the first floor; in the lower one he took advantage of the bubbles to be inhabited and a small *jameo* where the pool is located, everything communicated to each other by corridors excavated in the basalt and stepped of abundant vegetation. He left this house to move to Haría in 1988. He dedicated it as headquarters of his own Foundation which he had created himself in 1982 with a group of friends. The new headquarters of the Foundation was inaugurated in 1992 and it harbors a small museum of contemporary art, with his works and his particular collection.

He carries out several murals with volcanic stone for the *Arrecife Gran Hotel* in 1970 when he still was travelling and exposing. He finished the works of the watch tower of *El Río* in 1973.

In 1974 the Town council publishes him a book of pictures in white and black: "*Lanzarote, arquitectura inédita*" (Lanzarote, unpublished architecture). The work it picks up the existent popular architecture in that moment and it serves as base for his later work. He also opens up this year a the center in Arrecife, with cultural purposes, *El Almacén*; converted by the Town council, in 1989, in an Insular Cultural Centre. In 1976 he works in the project *Costa Martíanez* of the Puerto de la Cruz. He also inaugurates the museum installed in San José's Castle with a *Certamen Internacional de Artes Plásticas* (International Contest of plastic arts), after its restoration and adaptation. Likewise, he begins the works of *Jardín de Cactus* (Garden of Cactus).

Between this date and the year 1986 (year in which he was granted in London the *Premio Europa Nostra* (Europe Nostra Award) for his work in favor of the preservation of the environment, César Manrique lives some moments of great activity as well as of recognition to his work, so much inside as outside of Lanzarote. In this period he carries out works so significant as the *Banderas del Cosmo* (Flags of the Cosmos) and the atmosphere for the inauguration of the *Centro Astrofísico Roque de los Muchachos* (Roque Astrophysic Centre of the Boys), in La Palma. He designs the gardens and the pool of *Las Salinas Hotel* in Costa Teguise. He carries out the project for *La Vaguada* Commercial Centre (Madrid 1983); the view place of the *Palmarejo* (La Gomera, 1992). He receives the Gold Medal to the Tourist Merit; the World Prize of Ecology and Tourism of Berlin; the Medal of Gold of fine arts for the Government of Canary; the Goslarer Mönchenhaus-Preises for the Art and the Ecology granted by the city of Goslar and the Award Fritz Schumacher by the University of Hanover, in Germany; the Great Cross to the Civil Merit granted by King Juan Carlos; and, the Netherlande Honors D'Abeod in Holland.

From 1987 up to 1992 he finishes the *Jardín de Cactus* (Garden of Cactus); the Auditory of *Los Jameos del Agua*; he was named member of the Spanish Committee of the Program the Man and the Biosphere of the UNESCO. He works in the preliminary design of the Marine Park of the Mediterranean, in charge by the City council of Ceuta; and, he carries out the Pavilion of Canary for the Expo' 92 in Seville.

He died in a traffic accident the day 25 of September, 1992 at fifty meters of his Foundation.

Jameos del Agua. Work carried out by Jesús Soto and Luis Morales on César Manrique's idea. It was the first built tourist attraction of Lanzarote, in 1968. It consists on the adaptation, for the tourist exploitation, of one of the final parts of the volcanic tuff of the Atlantis in *Malpaís de la Corona*. Of its geologic formation, natural structure and endemic fauna we have already spoken previously in the section of Natural Areas: Place of Scientific Interest of the Jameos, for that we will only speak about the construction.

To enter in the *Jameo Chico* you need to go down using the stone stairway. The *Jameo Chico* became a bar-restaurant, and by descending a little more, one can have access to a tunnel of 21 m. high, and 19 m. wide, and 22 m. long. It contains a small lake of salted water connected with the sea, being influenced by the movement of the tides. The lake is not very deep but it looks like due to the reflection of the roof in the water. This is the habitatr of the *jameito* hábitat (see page 50 for more details). A greaat hole can be appreciated from which the light penetrates, formed in an explosion of gas when entering the lava in contact with the salted water. The incident light forms spectacular effects of colors when being reflected on the crystalline water. The lake is crossed by a passageway built in its lateral that leads us to a stairway that ascends to the *Gran Jameo*, of 100 m. long, and 13 m. wide, transformed into an exuberant garden with pool of blued water. On the bottom of this *jameo*, the tunnel opens up the way to an auditory with 600 seats and with an extraordinary acoustic. A singular auditory has been built where concerts and shows are carried out. It belongs to the National Network of Spanish Theaters.

Ascending from another zigzag stairway, a vulcanologic museum can be reached in the Big *Jameo*, the one denominated *Casa de Los Volcanes* (House of The Volcanoes), where they tell us the geologic processes that gave place to the birth of the island. It has a library with a deposit of 40 books, 5 thematic audiovisual, 598 offprint, and 30 videos; a multi-function assembly hall with all equipment type; room of monitors and geo-dinamic station, with information of the whole volcano world history; meeting room; and a main room with a permanent exhibition on these topics. It can be visited every day, from 11:00 to 18:00 hours.

Everything livened up with a very appropriate music, tropical and autochthonous vegetation and ornamental elements very well distributed. We comes out from where we have entered.

Interior pool of the Jameos del Agua.

Sculpture dedicated to the Fecundity.

Monument to the Peasant. Group formed by the Fecundity sculpture designed by César Manrique; constructions of popular imitation; and surroundings that emulate the *majorera* traditional life. It is located in the geographical center of Lanzarote, next to Mozaga.

The abstract sculpture has fifteen meters high and it is formed by tanks of water of old fishing ships welded to each other and colored with white. It was carried out by Jesús Soto and it represents a peasant with his herd.

Casa Museo (Museum House) was opened to the public in 1978. It reproduces the most typical in the rural popular architecture; central patio, reservoir, chimneys, balconies, oven, *tahona*, presses of wine and workshops. Everything very spotless, with colored wood of seafaring green. The group consists of bar, store of craft; ceramic shops, pottery, spun, and carpentry; museum of craft and peasant utensils; and restaurant, where all kinds of traditional plates are cooked.

The works with camels and donkeys can be seen in the surroundings of a rural field.

Cave of Los Verdes. The same as for the *Jameos del Agua* (we will only add some notes on the architectural intervention). The rest already counts it in Natural Places: Natural monument of *La Corona*.

Jesús Soto adapted the Cave for his visit in 1964. In this case the intervention, to which the space has undergone, is quite respectful. In the interior the only manipulation consists in the illumination system, perfectly camouflaged, and in the access paths. Therefore the natural phenomenom can be appreciate in all its splendour. The illumination enhances the chromatism of the walls and it causes sensational reflects in the water. Also the music give to the place a startling aspect, transforming it into one of the most attractive places in Lanzarote. At certain point of the inside, for its dimensions, an auditory is installed for some special occasions but it isn't out of place with the rest.

The additional services are: a small receptción-box office, with an access directly to the interior by a front step staked with vegetation.

Restaurant El Diablo. It is located in the Island of Hilario, inside the National Park of Timanfaya, and it is previous to the declaration of this area as Natural Park.

It was built in 1970, also under César Manrique's supervision, in the point where the technical anomalies are more important. Such a characteristic is taken advantage for cooking the foods with natu-

Entrance to Cueva de los Verdes.

Watch-tower of El Río.

Logo of César Manrique for the National Park of Timanfaya.

ral heat and some other show in the surroundings. The kitchen has a hole of six meters deep, in a chimney form, from where the heat goes up until a grill which reaches 300° C.

For its construction, stone, iron, and glass were only used to be able to support the high temperatures of the place. The building has a circular shape. The dining room opens up to the lava field through an immense window. It has a central patio, also round and crystal, where decorative elements have been placed: a fig trunk and portions of a calcinated dromedary skeleton which takes part of a legend on the place. The floor is isolated by special tiles.

The group, with great harmony, has a craft and souvenir shop, and other services of the Park.

Mirador del Río (watch-tower of El Río). This watch tower in *Famara* and *Chinijo* archipelago is located in the place of an old battery of canyons used during the war between Spain and United States for the sovereignty of Cuba at the end of last century.

On Fernando Higueras' project which was not end up carrying out, César Manrique suggests him the idea of the watch tower. Once accepted this new project, the watch tower began to be built in 1973 ending the following year.

The construction consists on a platform excavated in the cliff, at 479 m. high on the sea level, on the one that two huge domes have been built communicated to each other and later on buried to hide its construction. The domes are open to the cliff with two big windows. In its lateral side there are two doors opening the way to a terrace in overhang form. They are decorated with two big sculptures of César Manrique hanging down the roof, by way of lamps or motives. They were carried out in the same place and it was used old foils welded to metallic bars. A chimney of volcanic stone is located in one of the lateral side, and in the center, a circular stairway that leads to a terrace. The entrance to the building is carried out through a serpentine passageway. The facade has a wall of volcanic stone divided in three levels which hides the construction totally.

Jardín de Cactus (Garden of Cactus). Located in the outskirts of Guatiza, in the way to Mala. It is without a doubt a homage to this area dedicated during more than one century to the cultivation of the *tunera* to raise cochineals.

It is, again, a landscape intervened architecturally by César Manrique taking advantage of a *rofe* (volcanic ash) abandoned last century. Inaugurated in 1989, it is the last great work of the City council dedicated to the tourism. It has a form of amphitheater of big dimensions surrounded by tiers or staggered parterres covered with lapillus and gang-

Garden of Cactus.

planks of volcanic stone to facilitate its visit. The central part follows the same line, although here the flowerbeds have biggest dimensions and with stone monoliths completing the decoration. The building has the characteristic services of the exploitation: a bar-restaurant and a mill. Everything in perfect harmony. In the exterior there is the author's metallic sculpture, in form of giant cactus, of eight meters high.

This building harbours around 10.000 plants belonging to some 1.400 different species between cactus and gross plants.

PRACTICAL INFORMATION

Visas. Citizens of most countries do not need a visa to enter Spain.

Here, we will give some of the current regulations as outlined in the "Basic Regulations for the Control of Spanish Borders. National Police Office. Madrid, February 20th 1992". These regulations may be affected by subsequent treaties and international agreements.

The countries whose citizens require a visa to enter Spain are: Saudi Arabia, Algeria, Australia, Bahrein, China, United Arab Emirates, Philippines, Hong-Kong, Malasya, Morocco, Oman, Qatar, Tunisia, Venezuela and North Yemen, with the exception of those holding diplomatic passports. Travellers in transit are permitted 48 to 72 hours with an entry permit or on group tours. Visas can be obtained in Spanish embassies of the countries of origin.

Visas are not required for stays less than 90 days as long as the visit is not for business and the required documents are presented such as for: children under 14 years old, crews of boats and planes, residents of bordering territories, holders of residence permits, and student ID cards.

Citizens of the following countries, may enter Spain using their National Identity Cards: Germany, Andorra, Antilles Holland, Austria, Belgium, Denmark, France, Greece, Holland, Ireland, Italy, Liechtenstein, Luxembourg, Malta, Monaco, Portugal and Switzerland.

On entering Spain, visitors may be required to prove that they have sufficient funds to pay for their stay and a return ticket or passage to another country.

In case of doubt, readers should contact, by telephone if wish, the nearest Spanish embassy or consulate for further information or possible changes in the mentioned regulations.

Custom. We will try to summarise and to clarify some terms to facilitate the step customs officer.

According to the Department of Customs and Duties, a traveller is a person who temporarily enters Spanish territory.

When the purpose of a visit is not a commercial activity, the goods to which custom's regulations apply include everything in the personal luggage of the traveller. In addition to clothing and toiletry, personal effects include jewellery, photography, and video equipment, musical instruments, radios, cassette recorders, and the like, typewriters and calculators, portable televisions and computers, sports equipment (bicycles, surf boards and wind-surf, delta wing kites, skis, rackets, canoes, etc.), tents, camping equipment, fishing equipment, and similar items. Merchandise whose importation is prohibit is excluded.

Custom inspection could be selective or by random. As a general rule, travellers must give a verbal declaration of the goods they are carrying.

Citizens of EC countries are not subject to import restrictions on entering the Canary Islands. Citizens of third countries, Ceuta or Melilla, must pay duty on imports exceeding a value of 45 ECUs (6.200 pts) per person, and 23 ECUs (3.200 pts.) for children under 15 year old.

The value of goods is determined by the purchase receipt.

For certain products, quantity restrictions apply:

a) For ECC citizens:
- Alcoholic beverage:
  - over 22% vol. 1.5 litres.
  - not over 22% vol. 3 litres.
- Mild wine 5 litres.
- Perfume 75 grams.
- Cologne 3/8 litres.

b) For citizens of third countries:
- Cigarettes 200 units.
- Cigars 50 units.
- Tobacco 250 grams.
- Alcoholic beverages:
  - over 22% vol. 1 litre.
  - not over 22% vol. 2 litres.
- Perfume 50 grams.
- Cologne 1/4 litres.
- Coffee 500 grams.
- Tea 100 grams.

Minors under 17 years old don't benefit of this rank .

For temporary imports of none personal items, further documentation is required (ATA application form and community printed matter).

For exports, as a general rule, no documentation is required of travellers. Exceptions:

Firearms: subject to Administrative Importation (following presentation at customs) or Exportation Authorisation, and Civil Guard Firearms Control.

Pets: an Official International Certificate is required.

CITES (Protected Species): It must be presented CITES import and export documents for the affected countries.

Medicine: only personal medication is permitted without the previous action from the Health Department of the Island.

Works of Art: subject to presentation of a permit from the Office of Fine Arts and Archives, though works not requiring a permit are allowed to pass. In the case of works of living artists not exceeding one million pesetas in value, a *Solicitud de Salida* (Pass permit) from the Professional Association of Art Galleries will serve as a permit if stamped by the Office of Fine Arts and Archives.

The movement of foreign currency or pesetas across de border, whether is cash, bank notes, or bank checks, entering or leaving the country, need not to be declared as long as the total amount does not exceed one million pesetas per person per trip.

Any person can enter or leave with an ECC registered car, and since January 1st 1993 there is no restriction whatsoever on cars registered in the Canary Islands. Cars maybe imported temporarily from other countries, and in such cases a tourist registration is required.

The same regulations apply to recreational embarkation.

For more information contact: *Administración de Aduanas de Lanzarote* (Custom Administration). Address: Puerto de los Mármoles, s/n. Tel: 81 11 36 and 81 59 74.

Currency. The peseta is Spain's unit of monetary exchange, existing in coins of 1, 5, 10, 25, 50, 100, 200, 500 and 2,000 pesetas and bank notes of 1,000, 2,000, 5,000, 10,000 pesetas.

Money can be changed at the airport on arrival: at banks in the morning: in hotels (for clients only); and at exchange offices, usually found in tourist areas. The same applies to traveller checks. Any exchange transaction requires a passport (or identification card for travellers who do not need passports).

Credit cards are extremely useful and recommended. Automatic bank machines are located throughout the island, and credit cards are widely accepted in hotels, restaurants, travel agencies and petrol stations. The most popular are Visa, MasterCard, American Express and Diner's Club.

Tourist Information.

The Tourist Information offices depend on the Tourism Council of the Insular Town Council of Lanzarote through the Patronage of Tourism.

There are Tourist Information offices in the airport, in Arrecife and in Puerto del Carmen (Tías).

It can be useful to go by. They have general information on the island.

The travel agencies and some hotels' receptions have pamphlets about trips, schedules of flights, ships and buses "*guaguas*" modernised; also on activities and sport facilities.

Patronage of Tourism:
- Blas Cabrera Felipe, s/n. (Marine way).
35500 Arrecife.
Tel.: (34 28) 81 17 62; Fax (34 28) 80 00 80

Tourist Information:
- José Ramírez Cerdá Park. Arrecife.
(Generalisimo Franco Avenue, s/n).
Tel.: (34 28) 80 15 17.
- Avenida de las Playas, s/n.
Puerto del Carmen, Tías.

Travel Connections.

By air. Lanzarote's present airport handles both national and international traffic. Located 4 km. from Arrecife, the capital. The airport received 3.920.000 passangers in 1996.

The group Iberia, in regular flights, unites the island with Barcelona, Bilbao, Fuerteventura, Gran Canaria, La Palma, Tenerife, Madrid, Málaga and Seville. The frequency of these flights depends on the time of the year.

There are also regular flights with **Germany** (Berlin, Bremen, Colony, Bonn, Dresden, Dusseldorf, Erfurt, Frankfurt, Hamburgo, Hanover, Leipzig, Munster, Nuremberg, Saarbrucken, Stuttgart); **Belgium** (Brussels); **Finland** (Helsinki); **Austria** (Salzburg, Linz); **France** (Mulhouse); **Switzerland** (Basle), and **Denmark** (Copenague).

The charter airlines carry out flights from Alicante, Barcelona, Bilbao, Fuerteventura, Gran Canaria, Madrid, Málaga, Seville, Tenerife, Valencia, Valladolid and Vitoria. And in international flights from **Germany** (Berlin, Bremen, Colony, Bonn, Dresden, Dusseldorf, Erfurt, Frankfurt, Hamburg, Hanover, Leipzig, Munster, Nuremberg, Saarbrucken, Stutgart, Paderborn); **Portugal** (Lisbon, Port wine); **France** (Molhouse, Paris); **United Kingdom** (Belfast, Birminghan, Bristol, Cardiff, Glasgow, Liverpool, London, Luton, Manchester, Newcastle); **Italy** (Bologna, Rome, Verona); **Denmark** (Copenhagen); **Ireland** (Cork, Dublin); **Austria** (Vienna, Salzburg); **Switzer**land (Basle, Geneva, Zurich); **Norway** (Oslo, Bergen); **Czech Republic** (Prague); **Sweden** (Stockholm, Gothenburg); **Finland** (Helsinki) and **Morocco** (Marakech).

There are all kinds of services in the airport (buses, currency change, restaurant, tourist information, taxis, rent of cars, information of regular flights, information of flights charters, police, shipping, courier, stores, etc…).

Airport telephone: (34 28) 81 14 50
Iberia Office:
Rafael González Avenue, 2. Arrecife.
Tel.: (34 28) 81 03 58.

By sea. The port of Arrecirfe is the main port of the island as for goods and passengers. The *Compañía Transmediterránea* unites Arrecirfe with Las Palmas de Gran Canaria, Santa Cruz de Tenerife and Puerto del Rosario in Fuerteventura, three days a week. There is also a weekly itinerary with Cádiz, in the Península.

From Playa Blanca to Corralejo (Fuerteventura) there are five daily combinations with the ferry *Buganvilla* and six more with the ferry *Volcán de Tindaya.*

There are connections from Orzola to Caleta del Sebo (La Graciosa) three times daily with *Líneas Marítimas Romero.*

- *Transmediterránea*:
José Antonio street, 90. Arrecife.
Tel.: 81 10 19 - 81 08 21. Fax: 81 23 63.
- *Lineas Fred. Olsen: Ferry Buganvilla*
Muelle Playa Banca (Yaiza).
Tel.: 51 72 66
- Naviera Armas S. A.: Ferry Volcán de Tindaya.
Muelle (Wharf) Playa Blanca (Yaiza).
Tel.:.51 79 13. Fax: 51 79 12
- *Linea Marítimas Romero*
García Escaméz street, 11
35540 La Graciosa.
Te.: 84 20 55 - 84 20 70.   Fax: 84 20 69

On land. The recent vial network of Lanzarote is quite well conserved. It is constituted by a main and a secondary network, supplemented with earthy roads where the asphalt doesn't exist.

Buses cover all the points of the island, with abundant services for the day and for the most important towns, mainly for the tourist and the airport. For the smaller towns there are 2 - 3 daily services.

Pamphlet with the schedules are distributed through the centres of Tourist Information and travel agencies. We won't give details here due to extension and variability:

Highway from Yaiza to the National Park of Timanfaya.

Regular services of buses:

Lanzarote Bus. Tel.: 81 24 58 - 81 24 62

For some other information or necessity: *Guardia Civil* (type of police) telephone number is: 81 18 86.

Postal services. An acceptable and easy mail service exist in all the towns.

The central post and Telegraphs office is located in Arrecife:

Generalísimo Franco Avenue, n° 5.

Tel: 80 06 73 (in front of the Office of Information and Tourism of Paseo Marítimo).

Telephones. There is not any problem to this respect, so much for local calls as for international calls. There is a fine network of phone booths throughout the island, and telephone offices in the most populated areas. Service is provided for both local and international calls.

Health. The health while travelling largely depends on how well one takes care of oneself. Certain precautions should always be taken and adequate information obtained with respect to the types of ac-

tivities and risks involved: swimming, diving, hiking, etc. It is always best to be adequately prepared.

Travel insurance is recommended, to cover not only for loss and theft, but for health care as well. Some specifically exclude coverage for "dangerous activities", so it is necessary to be sure in advance on the extent of one's coverage.

It is not necessary to travel with a first-aid kit, unless special treatments are required, since there are plenty of pharmacies throughout the island carrying the full range of medications.

Vaccinations are not required. Climatic and hygienic conditions are perfect to a good health. Though adequate sun screen protection and a good hat are recommended for outdoor excursions.

The following is a list of Lanzarote's Public Health Centres.

Arrecife

- Lanzarote General Hospital.

Arrecife-Tinajo road. Km. 1.3. Tel.: 80 16 36. Hospital specialties: Cardiology, Pediatrics, Gynecology and Obstetrics, Surgery, Traumatology, O.R.L. Ophthalmology, Psychiatry, Internal Medicine.

- Valterra Public Health Centre.

Tel.: 81 63 58. General medicine, pediatrics.

Haría
- Haría Public Health Centre.
El Palmeral road, 6. 35520 Haría. Tel.: 83 56 21.
General medicine, pediatrics.
- Mala Public Health Centre.
Villanueva street, 39. 35543 Mala. Tel.: 52 95 16
General medicine, pediatrics.
Teguise
- Teguise Public Health Centre.
San Francisco square, 1. 35530 Teguise.
Tel.: 84 54 21. General medicine, pediatrics.
- La Graciosa.
Tel.: 84 20 27
Yaiza
- Yaiza Public Health Centre.
Yaiza-Playa Blanca road. Tel.: 83 01 90- 65
General medicine, pediatrics.
- Playa Blanca Public Health Centre.
Llegada avenue s/n. 35570. Tel.: 51 75 42.
General medicine, pediatrics.
San Bartolomé.
- San Bartolomé Public Health Centre.
Cerdeña Bethencourt street, 7. 35550
Tel.: 52 0261
General medicine, pediatrics and mental health.
- Playa Honda Public Health Centre.
San Borondón street s/n. 35509. Tel.: 51 0655
General medicine and pediatrics.
Tías.
- Tías Public Health Centre.
Tel.: 83 30 26.
General Medicine and pediatrics.
- Puerto del Carmen Public Health Centre.
Juan Carlos I street, 17. 35510. Tel.: 51 27 11
General medicine and pediatrics.
Tinajo.
- Tinajo Public Health Centre.
San Roque square, 3. Tel.: 84 04 45
General medicine, pediatrics.
- Santa Coloma Public Health Centre.
Tel.: 81 63 62
General medicine and pediatrics.

- Servicios de Urgencias (Emergency services).
Tel.: 80 44 70
In the tourist centers you also find private medical centers. And in all the mentioned populations pharmacies exist.
Good Health!

Accommodation. At present, the island has
accommodation with 65.000 hotel beds distributed in various tourist centers: Playa Blanca, Puerto del Carmen, Playa Honda, Arrecife and Costa Teguise, besides some other urbanization of apartments. All them in the coast.

All of these places are easily to find through travel agents, who have information on any kinds of available lodging. Most are of good quality, and most of them offer a high level of infrastructure.

For those who want to come to Lanzarote by themselves, we tell them that it is not difficult to find where to sleep. And if you want to leave from the tourist atmosphere, we will give you a list of economic lodgings and pensions. Although there are only some in Arrecife.

- Alespa. León y Castillo street, 56. Tel.: 81 17 56
- Arrocha I. Gómez Ulla street, 7 Tel.: 81 68 52
- Arrocha II. León y Castillo street, 98. Tel.: 80 24 21
- Cardona. 18 de Julio street, 11. Tel.: 81 10 08
- España. Gran Canaria street, 4. Tel.: 81 11 90
- San Ginés. Molino street, 9. Tel.: 81 18 63

Also, in most of the municipalities of the island are possible to rent houses or private apartments. These will allow you to be closer to the "*conejera*" community. You can find them through some agencies, at particular level, or through people that have already been in the island. If you are already in Lanzarote it is easier for you to take a walk around the chosen area.

Good Luck!

Rent of cars and bicycles. Offices
of rent cars exist in almost all the tourist centers of the island. Also in the travel agencies and the receptions of the hotels can give you information. There is not any problem to locate them and therefore it is not necessary to enumerate the agencies here with addresses and telephones.

The prices vary according to the vehicle's manufacturer, but at the same level of benefits, the prices are homogeneous in all the agencies. The cheapest oscillates between 4.000 *pesetas* and 5.000 *pesetas* per day and without km limits. If you rent a car for several days or weeks you can provably get a discount. Those four wheel cars (4 x 4) are something more expensive (approximately between 8.500 *pesetas* and 10.000 *pesetas*). You should use this type of vehicle if you want to leave off the highways. Otherwise you will have to take the responsibility of the damages caused to the car. It is obligatory an insurance, although the expenses of cranes go for the lessee's bill.

Travellers should inspect the vehicle's condition and read the fine print before concluding any rental agreement.

Driving on beaches is prohibited, not only by rental agencies (because of salt damage to cars), but also by the Environment Department.

Finally, we offer some advice concerning driving conditions on Lanzarote. Drive carefully on all roads, since many are very narrow and there are many rental cars on the roads. Stick to the main roads, for the good of the island, whether the use of secondary roads is prohibited or not. If one does choose to go off the main roads or onto the dunes, extreme caution is advised, if not for the good of the island, then for one's personal safety. Off-road accidents result in a number of deaths each year.

For the geographical characteristics of the island, almost completely plane, you can travel on bicycle. The distance are not very far but you should take cautions since the sun and the wind can make your trip a small disaster. The best system is when you are fan of sport and like travelling slowly through the places,.

If you have not brought your own bicycle, you can rent it in anyone of the tourist centers.

Sports.

All of the town councils offer a sports center, however modest, permitting the practice of a wide range of activities. Many hotels, and apartment complexes also feature sports facilities.

Vollyball, tennis, squash, stittles, ping pong, mini golf, gymnasium, jogging, swimming, ailing, waterskiing, and surfing are just some of the possibilities.

Hunting, in open season, and fishing (deep sea, coastal or underwater) are sports which, because of their environmental impact, have already been discussed in the section on ecology. Just as fishing techniques were listed in the section on the island's economy.

Two sports noteworthy for their spectacularity, and favoured by the conditions of the island, are diving and windsurfing. For this reason we include special information necessary for the practice of both sports.

Diving.

We will give a small orientation of the ocean characteristics for those that want to discover the secrets and curiosities of the marine bottoms, of the habitat, of the diving, and of the infrastructure with which you can count on while practicing this sport.

The oceanographic characteristics comes determined by the Current of Canary and the emerging of deep waters, rich in nutritious that take place in front of the African costs. This determines as much the temperature as the salinity of the water and therefore the flora and the characteristic of the fauna.

The tides are oceanic and with semi-diurnal regime, two high tide and two low tide for the lunar day. The biggest inter-tide width is 2.7 m. corresponding to the spring-tides of February and September.

Diving, therefore, is favoured by these conditions of temperature (17-23º C), visibility and acceptable transparency and the non-existence of dangerous species for the diver.

Two areas are distinguished clearly regarding marine bottoms; windward and leeward.

The windward areas, open to the dominant trade, presenting, most of the year, difficult conditions for the immersion. They are richer areas with marine species. The fishing has been traditionally less intense. Its bottoms are more interesting to the diver sport since these areas are more abundant in rocks, caves, and verges.

In the leeward areas, guided to the south, the sea presents some conditions of relative calm at any time of the year and it is where the best infrastructures for the diving are located.

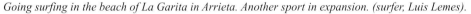
Going surfing in the beach of La Garita in Arrieta. Another sport in expansion. (surfer, Luis Lemes).

Diving centers.

- Atlántica Diving Center
  Roque del Este street, 1. Puerto del Carmen.
  Tel.: 21 01 27 Fax: 51 13 22
- Lanzarote Diving Center:
  Urb. Lanzatierra. Playa de las Cucharas.
  Costa Teguise. Tel.: 59 04 07
  Fax: 59 25 48
- Safari Diving School
  Playa de la Varilla (Varilla beach).
  Puerto del Carmen
  Tel.: 51 19 22 Fax: 51 04 96
- Calipso Diving
  Centro Comercial Calipso (Calipso Shopping
  Center). Avenue of Las Playas, s/n
  Costa Teguise. Tel.: 59 08 79
  Fax: 59 08 79
- Speedy Diving
  Playa Dorada Apartments.
  Tanausú street, 1. Pueto del Carmen.
  Tel.: 51 14 02
- La Santa Sport Diving
  La Santa (Tinajo).
  Tel.: 84 01 00 Fax: 84 01 52
- Las Toninas Diving
  Hotel-apartments Playa Flamingo.
  Playa Banca.
  Tel.: 51 73 69 Fax: 51 76 42
- Diving Equipment
  Avenue of Naos, 6. Arrecife.
  Tel.: 81 11 17 Fax: 80 03 46
- Barracuda Club Lanzarote
  La Geria Hotel. Playa de los Pocillos
  Puerto del Carmen. Tel.: 51 27 65
- Delfín Club
  Centro Comercial Aquarius (Aquarius Shop
  ping Center)
  Avenue of Las Playas, 38. Puerto del Carmen.
  Tel.: 51 42 90 Fax: 51 42 90
- Club Catlanza
  Puerto Calero. Tías.

Windsurfing. Given the sea and winds conditions, the coasts of Lanzarote are ideally suited for the practice of this sport. The most favourable areas are those of leeward being the windward beaches for the more experimented ones.

Windsurfing Centers:
- U.C.P.A.
Playa de las Cucharas. Costa Teguise.
Tel.: 59 07 96   Fax: 59 18 95

- Sport Away Center
  Playa de las Cucharas. Costa Teguise.
  Tel.: 59 19 74
- Centro de Windsurfing Nino Navarro
  (Nino Navarro Windsurfing Center)
  Playa de Matagorda. Puerto del Carmen.
  Tel.: 51 04 76
- Centro de Windsurfing Nathalie Simon
  Playa de las Cucharas. Costa Teguise.
  Tel.: 59 07 31 Fax: 59 07 31
- Centro de Windsurfing Club La Santa
  La Santa (Tinajo).
  Tel.: 84 06 24 Fax: 84 06 28

Gastronomy.

Gastronomy. For reason of climate and custom, Lanzarote's cuisine tends to be quiet plain. The main ingredients are fish and island produce flavoured with special sauces and seasoning.

Most Canary dishes are served with a centuries old island specialty known as *gofio*, made from toasted grain flour. *Gofio amasado* is made from a doughy mixture of *gofio*, water, milk, broth, potatoes, honey, wine etc., served in a *zurrón* (leather or fabric bag) or casserole dish. Most *gofio* is made with a mixture of toasted wheat and barley flour. Wheat and barley were one the island's most important crops. There is also *gofio de millo*, a course flour made from toasted corn.

Other dishes, served as appetizers, include:

Papas arrugadas, small unpeeled potatoes steam cooked with plenty of salt and served with mojo picón, a hot sauce.

Perjines, tiny fish of the sardine family, dried in the sun, then baked, grilled, or cooked in an alcohol flame.

Shellfish; mussels, limpets, and *burgaos* (gibbula canseis) steamed or in vinegar.

Crustaceous: crabs, small shrimps, spider-crab, and lobsters.

Optupus and roasted squid.

Braised *viejas jareadas*, fish cleaned, filleted, and dried for 24 hours, then grilled over hot coals.

Outstanding soups include; fish, potato with exploded egg, and *millo* (corn), as well as soups of hard bread and marrows or green *arvejas* (peas).

The most flavourful stews plows: Canary stew, with chickpea and kidney beans; and those made up of limpets, rabbit, hen, tongue, offals, cod, fried fish, chicken, mere in raw, octopus, pigeons, or kid. As example we will give the recipe of the made up of kid: it consists on chopping the kid, to put it in a brine and later on to fry it. Meanwhile some bread slices are fried and some garlic heads being wet a little to be also fried. Necessary water is set for the sauce, adding vinegar (a

Popular and quality restaurant in Arrieta.

little), pounded black pepper and chopped parsley. All this is boiled a little and then the kid is added. Exquisite!

The *baifo* meat "smeared" with *mojo picón* and fried; and the rabbit in *salmorejo* is the most typical and flavourful meats.

The fishes, for their abundance, prevails in the *majorera* kitchen and among them: the *sancochos* of *cherne* or *sama*, salting and boiled with potatoes and sweet potatoes that are dewed with *mojo picón*; the fiddle-fish with *mojo*, marine species of tender meat and well pleasure that it is consumed fresh or dry off; the parrot-fish, mullets, comber, white sea bream, fangtooth moray, etc., fried or parboiled and seasoned with oil and vinegar; And an endless list.

To finish the meal, anything better than a good dessert: pudding of flour of rice, plate of milk, sweet pineapples of almonds, "sighs" or pudding of cheese; that we know in this way; "To a pound of cheese, a pound of cow butter plus a pound of sugar plus 12 yolks of eggs and six egg white are added in to it, all of these are beaten well, place in a *pudinera* (pudding dish) and then placed in the oven".

If during the meal we have chosen a good wine of *La Geria*, the food will have been satisfactory. Good appetite!.

Pejines (Pejin fishes) drying off in the sun.

ARRECIFE

History. The surroundings of *Charco de San Ginés* were occupied by the aboriginal population. The conditions of natural port, protected for a barrier of islands and reefs, what led to the visitors of Lanzarote to use this enclave. Behind these islands: *Cruzes* (in front of *Puerto Naos*), French, *Castillo* and the *El Quebrado*, in the land area called *La Puntilla*, in the bank of *Charco de San Ginés*, a nucleus of fishermen settled down at the beginning of the XV century.

The first notices we have about this port dates in the year 1403 when it was used to bring provisions to Gadifer. In 1445, an agreement was reached among Diego de Herrera, Inés Peraza and the Catholic Kings to fortify a circular silo where to store goods and to build a paved ramp (the first pier in Arrecife). In 1477 it served as a base to Diego of Herrera for his expedition to Africa. One year later was Juan Rejón who used it and which name it still lasts for the place where his ship was tied up. In 1544, to defend of the external attacks, the outpost of *El Quemado* was built, and later on, San Gabriel's Castle (from 1574 to 1599). In 1630 the French merchant Francisco García Santellas erected a small hermitage in this place in honour to Saint Ginés. In 1771 the Saint José's Castle was finished built. In 1776, from 20 to 72 was the neighbors' increase, and then a chapel, some new factories, houses, cellars, boilers of distilling brandy and two ports were built; *Caballos Port* and *Naos* Port. In 1798 this hermitage becomes parish.

The birth like a city, at the beginning of the XIX century, are known in a detailed way thanks to D. José Agustín Alvarez Rixo, natural historian of this incipient municipality, and its "*Historia del Puerto de Arrecife*" (History of the Port of Arrecife). In 1802 there are already 1393 occupants among sailors, merchants, traders and workers. In 1821 the municipality is gotten; in 1847 the transfer of the Military Tribunal. And finally, in 1852 it reaches the insular capital city that Teguise flaunted, thanks to the important trade of the barrilla, the cochineal, and to the fishing fleet. The construction of its first commercial port was carried out in 1908. The last great development took place in the seventies with the arrival of the tourism.

General data. Arrecife total surface is 22,7 square km., being the smallest in the municipalities of Lanzarote. The municipal capital has an altitude of 20 m. on the sea level. Its total population is about 40,000 people. Population's entities that depend on Arrecife are: Los Alonsos, Altavista, Titerroy, San Francisco Javier, La Vega, Valterra, Casco, Las Salinas, El Cable, La Concha, Argana Alta, Argana Baja and Maneje.

The most significant local fiestas are: Saint Ginés, in August, the oldest in the island and considered of national tourist interest, with popular music, festival of *Havaneras* and competitions of *Vela Latina* (Candle Latin) traditional -rolled wafers of fishing that today they conform an autochthonous sport manifestation -, the Carnival, in February, and the *Corpus*, with their carpets of salt coloured by the downtown streets.

San José Castle.

Patrimony:

Castle of Saint José. It is built in 1779 choosing for such purpose a promontory of 8 m. on the sea level. It was projected by engineer Alfonso Ochando in times of Charles III. It has a semicircular plan on a base of ashlars of basaltic stone and mortar. It consists of two storeis, and due to the difference of the land, the main facade is in the upper floor. To enter, it is necessary to overcome a moat through a drawbridge that opens the way to a great room with barrel vault. From this room another similar one can be reached, superimposed to this, through a stairway. For another stairway located in front of the previous one you ascend to the terrace. Next to these naves they are other smaller outbuildings dedicated to warehouse, deposit of gunpowder, dungeons, and reservoir. In this building, after the reformation and adaptation in 1979, the International Museum of Contemporary Art was located. In this reformation an annex dedicated to bar restaurant where it can be reached from an interior stairway opened up by the reservoir; its wide windows opens to *Naos* and *Los Mármoles* ports.

In the interior, international artists' pictorial and sculptural works can be contemplated. It has 5 rooms. The main one is an auditory for the performance of chamber and contemporary music concerts. The 4 remaining rooms are located in the upper level. It can be visited every day from 11:00 to 21:00 h. Address: Puerto Naos s/n. 35.500 Arrecife. Tel.: 81 23 21.

San Gabriel Castle

Las Bolas bridge.

Castle of Saint Gabriel - Bridge of Las Bolas. It was began to be built in 1573 by Agustín de Herrera y Rojas command, being the captain's design Gaspar Salcedo. At the beginning it was an outpost with a square plan with four ramparts of diamond tip in their angles and wooden interior distribution. It was built in 1586 by the Algerian pirate Arráez Amurat who set on fire the castle before beginning the invasion on the island. From then the islet is called *El Quemado* (the Burned). In 1590, king Felipe II orders the Canary Islands' defense to an Italian engineer, Leonardo Torriani. He restructured the old fort and united the ramparts with a continuing wall with the purpose of enlarging the esplanade or square of arms. Between both walls are stuffed with rubbish that have been taken out nowadays in the restoration works, what is last a corridor around the castle. Also it counts with a room for the troop, a room for arms, a warehouse of gunpowder, and two reservoirs, everything with barrel vault. The castle was finished building in 1599.

The access to the castle was throughout the Bridge of Las Bolas, also projected by Torriani.

During the XIX century some repair works were made. Two canyons with caliber 24 which today were placed in the entrance. Starting from 1972 it was restored definitively to transform it into the Archaeological and Etnographic Museum. We can contemplate archaeology, ceramic, and ethnography pieces here mainly, distributed in six rooms in an irregular way. The schedule of visits is from Monday to Friday from 8:00 to 15:00 h. Tel.: 81 19 50.

Casa Agustín de la Hoz (Agustín de la Hoz's House). Changed into a Culture House. It is a perfect example of the residential architecture of Lanzarote. It can be visited from Monday to Friday from 9:00 to 13:00 and from17:00 to 20:00 h. Avenue of Generalísimo Franco, 7. It has 3 projection rooms and an exhibition room with 300 paintings.

Church of Saint Ginés. It was finished building in 1665 and later on it had several reformations. Churches are a good criterion for the growth of the city. It highlights its organ of tubes and its good acoustics for the celebration of concerts (coral and camera music). We can also contemplate the image of Saint

San Ginés Church.

Ginés, and Virgin of El Rosario (sculpture brought from Cuba by an anonymous captain), the Christ's image, and a great painting of *Ánimas* (Souls). It is finished off by a bell tower with three bodies ended by a hood and a wind vane.

Casa de los Arroyos (Arroyos' House). Also called Colonel Armas' House. It was built in 1739 by Domingo Armas Bethencourt, ship-owner and military governor of Lanzarote. His son will inherit the house and later on his granddaughter who married a member of the Arroyos' family. The architectural style is late for that time and it represents the domestic architecture of that time, being a clear exponent of the oldest constructions of the city. Only a part of the original building is contemplated today. The rest has left destroying by segregations of family inheritances.

At the present time the Town council of Lanzarote has recovered it as Blas Cabrera Felipe Scientific-Cultural Center with a permanent exhibition on this eminent scientific (Arrecife-México 1878-1945). You can also see his monument in *Paseo Marítimo* (the Marine promenade), next to the old Inn. *La Casa de Los Arroyos* has several more rooms for other exhibitions. Coll Avenue, 3 (in front of the Castle of Saint Gabriel).

Besides the described buildings, the followings also belong to the architectural and monumental patrimony: The **mill of the "Cabo Pedro"**, in Lomo de la Pedrera, in the high part of the city; the **housings** of

Fajardo street, numbers 5 and 6; the **Island Headquarter**, León and Castillo st. 6; and, the **joint-neighborhood of San Ginés**, next to Charco. Also the **Marina** urban spaces, from the hotel Arrecife until Charco; **Islote del Amor**, in front of *Reducto* beach; and **mills** and **salt flats** of Puerto Naos, between Puerto Naos and Saint José's castle.

Surroundings. The municipality is located in the center of the island, limiting to the south with Saint Bartolomé, to the west and north with Teguise and to the east with the sea. Its surface is very smooth. It is not affected by the recent volcanic eruptions, and it only highlights a series of mountains located in the west boundary. All of this facilitates the circulation of the *jable*, from west to east, pushed by the dominant winds. The most attractive thing, from the natural point of view, is the coast: formations of reefs that protect the coast, mainly in the capital.

Useful information:
City Hall: Vargas street, 1. 35500 Arrecife.
 Tel.: 81 27 57 - 81 04 52 Fax: 81 37 78 - 54
Public Library: Old Inn of Tourism, s/n.
 Open from Monday to Friday. From 9:30 to 13:00 h. and from 17:00 to 20:00 h.
El Aljibe Art Gallery (named **El Almacén**). José Betancort 33. Three exhibitions rooms.
Libraries: (Subject: Canary issues and Lanzarote).
 - Diama Library. León y Castillo street, 12.
 - El Puente Library. Luis Martín street, 11.
 Tel. and fax: 81 51 07
Local Police Station: Tel.: 80 29 94 - 81 13 17

San Ginés puddle.

HARIA

History. The history of this municipality is not very excellent. It has a past marked by the misery, the successive external invasions, and the emigrations at the beginning of this century. It is starting from the arrival of the tourism when it flourishes with more intensity.

Their name comes from a degeneration of the term *Faría*, from the time of the Conquest, but its pre-hispanic name is ignored. A neighborhood's record of 1587 accounts that there was a pile and about 80 to 100 people. In this time it was the only town of Lanzarote, plus the capital: Teguise. In 1590 Torriani narrated that there are not more than 1.000 inhabitants in the whole island, out of 250 are military, and forty horses; being so few people the reason of the three *razzias* in 16 years on the part of the Moorish and Turks pirates. The pirate attacks more devastating were those of Morato Arraéz's (or Amurat), in August of 1586, burning all the palms -by luck they sprouted in another time-; and the 1618 attacks in which the population was betrayed after taking refuge in the Cave of *Los Verdes*. In 1776, the population was already constituted with 1000 people, out of 300 were located in Máguez, and about 10 in Ye or Guinate. In 1900, the population changed over to 3.200 people, being already established a family in Arrieta and another in Punta Mujeres. The maximum population bench mark belongs to 4.500 people in 1950. The church was built in 1619 having, along the time, diverse setbacks. The storm in 1956 was the most important and only last the tower. The Asunción Virgin is the patron saint and her image was sculpted by Luján Pérez.

General information. Total surface is 106,6 sq. km., and total population is about 3.000 inhabitants. It occupies the NE. part of the island. The municipal capital has an altitude of 270 m. Population's entities that depend on Haría are: Arrieta, Charco del Palo, Guinate, Máguez, Mala, Orzola, Punta Mujeres, Tabayesco and Ye.

The most important local *fiestas* so much of the capital of the municipality as the diverse areas belonged are: Saint Juan (June 24th), Saint Pedro (June 29th), El Cristo de la Sed (The Christ of the Thirst) (July 1st), the Carnivals (February), El Pino (The Pine) (Semtember) and Saint Bárbara.

The palm craft highlights on the rest, being famous the baskets with *pírganos* (palm leaves); also those of reed and rosetta made by thread.

Patrimony. We will only enumerates the architectural and monumental patrimony as well as the prominent urban spaces: **Watch Tower of El Río**; **Cave of Los Verdes**; **Jameos del Agua** (these three are broadly described previously). The **Sacrum-Popular Museum** can be visited in León y Castillo square, from Monday to Friday, from 11 to 13 h. and from 16 to 18 h. It depends upon the Canary Diocese; **Church of Nuestra Señora de la Encarnación**; **Church of Saint**

Haría.

99

Juan, from the XVII century; **León y Castillo Group-Square**; **House** in Tegala street 1; **House of Paz Currás** in Jose Antonio street; **House of Antonio López Socas** in Angel Guerra street; **Casa of César Manrique**, in the north-east of the urban centre; **Craft workshop and store** in Longuera street, s/n. It can be visited from Monday to Friday form 9 to 13 h. and from 16 to 19 h. Shops (in operation) of macramé, ceramic, span, doll-making, rosettas, tablecloth, etc; all in Haría. **Saint Bárbara church** and **dwelling** in Morote street in Máguez. **Curbelo House**, in the coast, in front of the town; **Port**; and the **Maritime Promenade** of Arrieta. **Nuestra Señora de las Mercedes Hermitage** in Mala. **Port** and **Maritime Promenade** of Orzola and Punta Mujeres.

Curbelo's House.

Surroundings. It occupies the north of the island, only limiting with Teguise from the south. From geologic, agrarian, ecological, and landscaping point of view, the part of Lanzarote more diverse are: volcanic cones, *malpaises*, diverse types of agriculture , vegetable endemism, accumulations of sand, etc. It contains the only arboreal concentration of Lanzarote: the palm trees of Haría; the only experience of forest re-population in *Peñas de Chache*; spaces of exceptional tourist attractiveness as the *Jameos del Agua*, *La Cueva de los Verdes* and the *Mirador del Río*; the spectacular valleys of *Temisas*, *Tabayesco* and *Haría*; the cliffs of *Famara*; the *salinas of El Río*; *Risco* beach; the *malpaís* of *La Corona*; the volcanic group of *La Quemada*, *La Corona* and *Los Helechos*; their urban nuclei; the park of exotic birds of Guinate; besides other singular elements of great value.

Useful information.

City council: 83 50 09 - 83 53 00. Fax: 83 51 73
Information to the Consumer: 83 52 52
Local Library: 83 50 09
Local police: 83 52 51

Marine promenade in Punta Mujeres.

TEGUISE

History. The Real Villa of Teguise is one of the oldest population's establishments of the Canary islands. Therefore it has a wide history which we will try to summarise here.

The current Teguise rises on what was the prehispanic village of *Acatife*, denominated by the Europeans as "Great Village". It was a group of "deep" houses around a pond, sustenance for the *Gran Mareta,* built years later by Sancho de Herrera. It was founded at the beginning of the XV century and Maciot of Bethencourt resided in there with the princess Teguise, king's Guadarfía (Guadafrá) daughter, the last aboriginal king (1393) before the arrival of the conquerors. It was the main residence of the Canary Lors; the insular capital up to 1852; headquarters of the marquisate of Lanzarote, instituted by Agustín de Herrera (grandson of Sancho); and headquarters of the vicary. The first defensive rampart was ordered by Sancho of Herrera to be built and it consisted on a simple watchtower in the near mountain of *Guanapay*, where great part of the island and the marine horizon were sighted. During the XVI century it became *Santa Bárbara* castle. Although it was not enough to avoid the tragic consequences of the sporadic pirate attacks to the island. *Callejón de la Sangre* (Alley of the Blood) remembers the slaughters carried out by Amurat, in August 1596 on the inhabitants of the town. In 1596, it was a small town of little more than a hundred houses covered with canes and straw, with piece of mud hardened by the sun and a small church lacked of windows. In the course of the XVII century so much Berberisc pirates arrived that carried out its forays in the islands and coast of Africa; as European pirates, with an action field that reach India and the Caribbean. The church of Nuestra Señora de Guadalupe dates from the XV century and therefor its walls have suffered the weight of the recent history of Lanzarote. Plundered in the years 1569,71,86, 1618 and finally a fire in 1909 the parochial file was demolished. Together with the church, Dominics and Franciscans convents were founded. Starting from the middle of the XVII and XVIII centuries the church was rebuilt, maintaining the stamp of ecclesiastical and conventual city that had in those dates. Reviewing their architectural patrimony we can follow the successive steps of its history.

General Information. Its population is about 15.000 inhabitants, for a total surface of 264 sq. km. The capital's altitude is 305 m. on the sea level. Population's entities depending on Teguise are: Caleta de Famara, Las Caletas, Costa Teguise, Guatiza, El Mojón, Mozaga, Muñique, Nazaret, Soo, Tahiche, Tao, Teseguite, Tiagua, Los Valles, Caleta del Caballo, Los Cocoteros, Charco del Palo, and La Graciosa (Caleta del Sebo and Pedro Barba).

«... one of the most important architectural groups in Canarias...»

The agriculture is the main economic activity in the interior areas. Tourism is located mainly in the coast, being the traditional fishing in a second plane. Also the commercial wharf of *Los Mármoles* belongs to this municipality, the most important in the island.

The local festivities are: La Virgen del Carmen (July 16th), La Virgen de las Nieves (August 5th); and the Ranchos de Pascua (Easter Ranchs), they are Christmas folkloric manifestations.

As for the craft is concerning, the plam handcraft and the *timples* production are outlined.

Patrimony:

Castle of Santa Bárbara. Located in *Guanapay* Mountain, a castle from the XVI century. It can be reached from Arrecife-Teguise general highway. The previous structure was modified and reinforced, with a more defensive character, by Leonardo Torriani in 1590. It has a romboidal plan with two circular towers and strong masonry walls. Abandoned in the course of the time and it was restored for first time in 1960. In 1977, architect Alemany gave it the interior aspect that today we can see. Finally, in 1989 it was remodeled again to be transformed into the headquarters of the Emigrant's Museum. It can be visited from Tuesday to Friday from 10 to 15 h., on Saturdays

and Sundays from 11 to 15 h. and it remains closed on Mondays and holidays. Here we find documentary funds, graphical files, a specialized library, a bookstore, a store, a warehouse, and a room of conferences where diverse cultural activities are organized.

Parochial church (of Guadalupe). It was built by Maciot of Bethencourt carried out his uncle's command, the conqueror Juan of Behencourt. The exact construction date is ignored although it is known that it was already finished in times of Diego de Herrera around 1452. In 1674, after the successive destructions on the part of the pirates, it was reconstructed incorporating several chapels to it, paid by the families that had the right of being buried in them. Such it is the case of the biggest Chapel, belonging to captain Bartolomé de Cabrera. This new source of revenues will allow important reformations during the XVIII century, like for example the bell tower, with two choir-stall bodies and a square plan built in 1727. On the first body two wooden balconies are placed. The second one is smaller. Eight arches of half point are located where the bells are placed. It finished off by an octagonal dome recovered by wooden profile. In 1769 the wooden tip was finished and a clock was installed.

From 1818, the external structure and the columns had the current state. In 1863 the wooden altar-

Santa Bárbara Castle.

Parochial church of Guadalupe.

piece was built. In 1864, besides repairing the windows, all the altarpieces were painted. In 1865 the roofs of the three bodies were painted with oil technique and another altarpiece was built. In 1892 the iron handrails which separates the arches from the biggest Chapel were installed. And in 1894 the choir and the roof of the sacristy are repaired. February 6th, 1909, a fire destroyed everything leaving alone the facade. It is reconstructed with the same form by the parishioners.

Convent of Saint Francisco. Building from the XVI century (1588 - 1590) built under the initiative of Argote of Molina as lordy mausoleum for Sancho de Herrera. It is the ninth convent of the Franciscan order and in it the remains of the most illustrious people from Lanzarote rest . It was destroyed by the 1618 pirate invasion and reconstructed later on, except for the sepulchers of the lordy mausoleum. In 1705 the tower of the church was built. It passed to the civil power in 1835. In 1973, in a wasted restoration, the three wooden altars of the central hall, another from the lateral hall, altarpieces, and two pulpits were destroyed. At the present time only last the church with three altarpieces of Baroque style, one of them made with clear stone and masonry. Also, the wooden pulpit and the Pile of volcanic stone highlight for their size. It was reformed in 1984 to be transformed into the

Lateral bell-gable of San Francisco's Convent.

Municipal Exhibition Room. Periodic exhibitions of Contemporary Art can be contemplated. Open from Monday to Friday from 10 to 16 h; on Saturdays and Sundays from 11 to 15 h.; Tuesdays are closed.

Convent of Santo Domingo. Been founded in 1729 starting from captain Gaspar Rodríguez Carrasco's legacy for a hospital and foundlings' cradle to the Dominic order. The convent and the church constitute the architectural group that at present comprise the City Council and Santo Domingo church.

The building of the convent, after having suffered enough artistic violations, presents today a facade of double composition: a lateral bell-gable to the left, two doors of great size, and a glazed opening. On the right with red fore-edge they are the symbols of the Dominic order. Attached to the right lateral the volcanic stone chapel which lost the roof in the XIX century. Two bodies appear inside, one 36 m. long and 8 m. wide, and the other a little smaller. Separated to each other by four half point arches in red and black stone work. It is located in Saint Domingo square.

Hermitage of the Veracruz. Been founded in the XVIII century. Starting from 1841 it becomes a neighborhood, being the neighbords in charge of its maintenance. It has a rectangular plan, with a sacristy attached to its right side. At the corners, stone works of black stone appears. The two slopes' roof is made of wooden covered with plate of mud and festooned with a line of tiles. A wooden choir, a small carved pulpit from the XIX century, a baptismal pile made of volcanic stone, three altarpieces, and two paintings of great format are located inside. The Christ with greenish colour and natural hair was brought from Portugal in the XVII century.

Spínola Palace. Located in the main square. It was built in the old Inquisition site in 1730 - 1780. Built in a single plan with a stone entrance door and steps of figured black stone. Five windows and some big flowerpots in the eaves complete the facade decoration. A chapel, galleries, two patios with reservoir,

Torres's House.

kitchen and a granary are as well located. Two lions sculpted by a family member are placed in front of the facade. It has been recently transformed into a museum-house (Lordy house with furniture), and exhibition room. It is open from 9:30 to 14:30 h. except Wednesdays.

Diezmos House (cilla). From the first half of the XVIII century. Small building with a square plan and thick stone and mud walls, where the stored grains were collected by the ecclesiastical tithes. Located next to the Spínola's Palace and today is a headquarters of Caja Insular Bank.

Casa Torres. Located at the back of Spínola's Palace. Built in two stories, in the XVIII century. It has a central patio paved of pebble and reservoir, and a facade with wide steps railing finished of typical big flowerpots. The upper floor is surrounded by a wooden gallery, and the basements conserve some narrow loopholes with stone-working outside. The stone work roofs among torch beams are festooned by three lines of tiles. Its chimney with about three meters high combines with octagonal and cubic forms.

Herrera y Rojas' Palace. This small palace was built on a house, in the XVIII century. The facade made with a stone work arch has the inscriptions AH and Ms interpreted as Agustín de Herrera, Marquis located in José Bentacort street s/n. It can be visited in the mornings.

Hermitage of San Sebastián in El Mojón.

Historical Archive of Teguise (Perdomo House). House with a 500 sq.m. surface plan. It presents a facade with two windows and wide two doors. It has three living rooms and a central patio with a reservoir, among other dependences. The roofs are of torch made. Old Town council and Teguise City council details can be found in it. Located in Carniceria street, 8.

Moreover, in Teguise are located: **Casa Cuartel** (Barrack); **San Miguel square** (or the *Los Leones*); **Historic built-up** area; **Parochial House** with neoclassical windows in the facade; **Jiménez House**; **Molino** (Mill) ; and **Casa Correos** (Post Office). Today it is a nursery home.

Las Nieves Hermitage.

Corazón de María Hermitage (Caleta de la Villa) in La Caleta wharf.

Communal - Town (Costa Teguise).

Saint Sebastian Hermitage (El Mojón). Popular hermitage with Mudéjar roof, built in the XVI century. It has four popular images.

Hermitage of Saint Catalina (Los Valles). Dated on the XVIII century. It is also a popular hermitage with Mudéjar roof. We can contemplate inside 4 paintings from the XVIII century, 3 popular images (Saint Catalina, Saint Antonio and the Sacred Christ), and an image attributed to Estévez.

Saint Leandro Hermitage (Teguise). Built in the XVIII century. The Mudéjar roof is located in there, as the ones with the same style. 2 Baroque altarpieces, the image of Saint Leandro and the Virgin's image are found as well. Located in San Leandro square.

Saint Juan Evangelista Hermitage (Soo). Built in the XVII century. It has 3 wooden images.

Nuestra Señora del Socorro Hermitage (Tiagua). Dated from the XVI century. A popular her-

Hermitage of San Leandro in Teseguite.

Mill and Molina in El Patio.

farming tools, two Wind Mills as well as the performed projections can be contemplated. It is open from Monday to Friday, from 10 to 17:30 h. and on Saturdays from 10 to 14:30 h.

Hermitage of Saint Andrés (Tao). Popular hermitage of Mudéjar roof with two naves: one of the XVIII century and the other of the XX century. We can contemplate a popular Baroque altarpiece and 2 wooden images.

Saint Lucía Hermitage (Mozaga). Built with wooden roof in the XIX century. A popular Baroque altarpiece and the image of the Virgin of La Peña can be admired in there.

Hermitage of Nazaret (Nazaret). A hermitage, from the XVII century, with Mudejar roof, a Baroque popular altarpiece, two wooden images, and a silver lamp,.

Hermitage of Santiago (Tahiche). Built in the XVII century, with similar characteristic to all those of its type. Two paintings and Santiago's popular Baroque image can be seen in there.

Hermitage of Saint Margarita (Guatiza). Built, in the XIX century, in a Canary neoclassical style. A painting of Souls and a restored organ from the XIX century; as well as an altarpiece of Saint Margarita (s. XVII) can be seen in there. It is also worshipped the Christ of Las Aguas. It is finished off with a glazed lantern.

Molino (Mill) (Guatiza). Inside of the *Jardín de Cactus* (Garden of Cactus).

Zonzamas Archaeological deposit of ore . With "cheesemaker and cyclopean constructions." Located in San Bartolomé road direction to Tahiche.

mitage of Franciscan influence. A stone altarpiece, two wooden images, two paintings, and a silver lamp are located in there.

Agricultural Villa Museum "El Patio" (Tiagua). Built in 1790. In 1845 the activity begins as agricultural property where tobacco was planted. One century later becomes the biggest property in Lanzarote with more than 40 workers and 25 camels. It was abandoned after the agricultural crisis. A member of the family began the reconstruction in 1980 concluding in 1994 when it was opened up to the public. Traditional

Surroundings.

The islets, called *Archipiélago Chinijo* from the north of the island, belong to the municipality of Teguise. Respect to the island, it limits to the north with Haría and to the south with Arrecife and Tinajo. It is compound by a valley of *Tenegüime*, the extensive surfaces of sand *(jable)* that cross the municipality from the *Famara* beach, some of the volcanic eruptions from 1730 - 36, or the *Tao's* volcano. But the cliffs of *Famara* are the most outstanding in its orography belonging to the latest eruptions of Lanzarote from 1824.

Useful information.

City Council: Tel.: 84 52 26 - 84 50 01 - 84 50 74. Fax: 84 50 59.

Natural Center Gallery: 18 July square, 8. Open daily from 10 to 14 h. and from 17 to 20 h. Tel.: 84 55 02

Historic Archives: Carnicería street, 1. Open from Monday to Friday from 9 to 13 h. Tel.: 84 54 67.

Local Museum: Tel.: 84 51 81 - 84 53 73.

Hermitage of Saint Margarita, in Guatiza.

SAN BARTOLOMÉ

History. The history of this city is quite less significant. *Ajei* was called by the old island inhabitants. The only historical facts to be pointed out is due to the consequences of the advance of the jable. That made the people to go back to places more secure. Another important fact is due to a family that represented the authority of Lanzarote during the second half of the XVIII century. This family in question is Don Francisco Guerra Clavijo y Perdomo's family: Sergeant-Mayor Gerra, Lieutenant Colonel and Chief of the Provincial Regiment of Lanzarote Militias, court-officer and Dean of San Bartolomé's City council. He died on February 3rd 1808, causing his death a hereditary succession problem among his son, Lorenzo Bartolomé Guerra and José Feo de Armas, natural of Teguise and heir of the Spínola palace. The dispute was solved under coercion and in favor of José Feo after an insurrection in Arrecife in 1810. José Feo resigned afterwards. The new appointed General Captain of Canary and President of the Regional Audience, the duke of the Park established the norm which the superior control of the militias should not relapse in any island inhabitant.

The church was founded in 1787 by Cayetano Guerra, brother of the Sergeant-mayor. It was taken up as Parish in 1796. This place begins to work as city council in the first third of the XIX century.

Church of San Bartolomé.

General information. Approximate population of 7.000 inhabitants in an extension of 40,9 sq. km. The capital altitude is 240 m. on the sea level. The populations that depend on San Bartolomé are: Güime, El Islote, Montaña Blanca and Playa Honda.

The main economy activity was the agriculture at the beginning as municipality. But this activity has changed into the service sector, especially the construction and the tourism, due to the arrival of the tourism, and only 6 km. distance far from the capital. The prevailed agriculture is on sanded so much in the *jable* (onions, vegetables,...) as in volcanic areas (vineyards).

As for the craft, the palm Works, the rosettas, and fittings highlight. The musical folklore is broadly represented by the grouping Ajei, which we have already spoken.

The most important festivities are: Saint Bartolomé (August 24th), Saint Elena (August 18th), and the Summer Final *Fiesta* in Playa Honda.

Patrimony:
Ajei Cultural House. It is in the General Franco street and it is an old elegant building of farm from the XVIII century. It opens from Monday to Friday, from 17.00 to 22.00 h.

Saint Bartolomé Church. Built in 1789. It conserves an altarpiece from the XVIII century and Saint Andrés' sculpture, and a Crucified.

Chimney.

Rural atmosphere in the streets.

Mayor Guerra house and a **Mill** in San Bartolomé. **Monument to the Peasant** (Mozaga) and the **Mill** of Güime.

Surroundings. The municipality is located in the central part of the island. Limited to the north with Teguise; to the west with Tinajo; to the south with Tías; and to the east with Arrecife and the sea, among *Piedra El Bajal* in Playa Honda and the beach of *Guasimeta*. The facilities of the airport are divided by its boundaries.

The territory is quite plane, standing out some volcanic cones belonging to different series: *La Mina*

(442 m.), *Guatisea* (544 m.), or *Juan Bello* (430 m.). To the north of the municipality the *jable* extends reaching the sea coming from the costs of *Famara*. The west is occupied by the lava of *Timanfaya*, where we can see, besides important geologic formations, the plantations of vineyards on sand bank and have more than enough cracks in the lava: area of *Juan Bello* mountain. In Masdache highway to San Bartolomé are several wine cellars of these vineyards.

Useful information:
City Council: 52 13 12 - 52 12 00.

Museum House of the Monument to the Peasant.

Juan Brito in his workshop at the Monument to the Peasant.

TINAJO

History. The Inaguadén farm, one of the most productive of the Count of Lanzarote, was settled in this municipal boundary. Ana Viciosa, the daughter of Juan de Saavedra (brother of the Count) and wife of the governor Juan de León Mungía, lived and controled these lands and a hundred of inhabitants toward 1650. The title and Montaña Clara's property was granted to her by the marquess of Lanzarote's will. These lands, due to the devastating consequences of the volcanoes, have been grasses'areas for livestock until the definitive later agricultural demarcation.

The hermitage, dedicated to Saint Roque is already figured in 1679, being enlarged in 1738. It was classified as second parish in 1792.

Tinajo acquires its independence as municipality on January 26th, 1802.

General information. An extension of 290 sq. km. with a population of about 4.000 inhabitants. The capital altitude is 195 m. The towns that depend on Tinajo are: El Cuchillo, Mancha Blanca, La Santa and Vegueta.

It is an eminently agricultural municipality and all type of "*conejeros* cultivations" are given: in topsails, in the *jable*, in natural and artificial san-bank and, in the area of *El Quemado*, in holes made in the lava

areas. At the present time, the service area is taking more and more importance due to the tourist centers of La Santa and Timanfaya.

Besides the works in palm and hats, we have mentioned here the work of the old potter Mrs. Dorotea with her descendants and successors to highlight the craft of this area

The most important festivities are: September 15th, commemorating Dolores's Virgin and where different historical facts are represented: August 16th, festivity of Saint Roque; and the Corpus, in which the streets around the square are colored with salt where the procession pass by the following day.

Patrimony:

Dolores Church (Mancha Blanca). Built in 1780. The origins start with a promise formulated by the people jointly to the Virgin so that she stopped the advance of the lava toward Tinajo. The same thing happened when the volcano extinguished on Julio 31st 1824 due apparently when the people took the Virgin out the street. The Dolores's Virgin or *Nuestra Señora de los Volcanes* (Our Lady of the Volcanoes), as she is known locally, is the patron saint of Lanzarote and in her honour two festivities take place per year: The Dolores's day, in September; and the other on July 31st, *Fiesta del Fuego*, because of the volcano history. The current structure is similar to the primitive

Church of San Roque in Tinajo.

Church of Los Dolores in Mancha Blanca.

one. It has been added the dome, bell tower, choir, and the houses of the pilgrims and the *"santero"* (superstitious worshipper). The church was restored in 1861.

Church of Saint Roque (Tinajo). Located in the square of the same name. It was built with Mudéjar roof in 1795. The altar-piece highlights in the interior with a Christ attributed to Luján Pérez, and a Virgin of Candelaria made by Fernando Estévez, pupil of Luján.

Hermitage of Nuestra Señora de Regla (La Vegueta).

Surroundings. The municipality is located in the western center of the island. Limited to the east with Teguise, San Bartolomé and Tías; to the south with Yaiza; and to the west with the sea. The coastal fringe, in a large part, is the *malpaís* of Timanfaya. A little more to the north some sandy beaches inserted between soft cliffs and rocky costs are located. The sand areas only appear in an artificial way in the Isle, earth tract separated by *El Río* and where the facilities of La Santa complex are located. The rest of the municipal term is buried by the lava from 1730-36 eruptions and those from 1824. We will highlight the alignments of calderas as: *Caldera del Corazoncillo, Señalo, Los Rostros, Rilla* and *Los Rodeos*; The *Rostros, El Cortijo, Caldera Quemada,* and *Montaña Quemada*; and, *Ortiz, Colorada* and *Negra*. The islets left by the lava are also interesting to see. Some are small as *Gato,*

Los Camellos, or *Los Dises*; and others are enormous as *Caldera Blanca, Teneza* or *Tinache.*

Useful information.

City council: San Roque square, 8. Tinajo.
   Tel.: 84 00 21 - 84 02 73
Municipal library tel.: 84 02 12

Hermitage of Nuestra Señora of Regla in La Vegueta.

TÍAS

History. The urban nucleus was formed around some farmers' houses. The name Tías (aunts) comes from the origin of these farmers' families. Therefore, around the houses of the Molina's family was formed the neighborhood of the low part, which where today the general highway passes through. The same thing happened with Robayna's family in the high part, and with the Fajardo's family. These three groups of houses ended up forming only one unit with the name of Tias de Fajardo (Fajardo's Aunts). But finally it has lost the last name. Mrs. Francisca and Mrs. Hernán Fajardo were direct aunts of Don Alonso Fajardo (Governor of Gran Canaria). They were single and matrons of the old dominion. The union of these groups is very irregular for what is a dispersed town. The development of Puerto del Carmen, formerly La Tiñosa, in the last years, has eclipsed the old downtown of Tías and other municipality nuclei.

General information. A 64,6 sq. km extension and 200 m capital altitude from 10 km. to Arrecife. The total population is about 8.000 inhabitants. The following populations depend on Tías: La Asomada, Conil, Mácher, Masdache, Puerto del Carmen and Vega de Tegoyo.

Tourism is the municipality main economic source. The agriculture is for subsistence, and the wine production of La Geria only highlights.

The most important festivities are: La Candelaria (February 2nd), the Carnival and the festivity of the Carmen (first Sunday of August).

Patrimony. Th architectural patrimony is summarized in the following constructions: **Casa Pascacia; Molino; Church of the Virgin Nuestra Señora de la Candelaria**, built in 1796, it is located

Church of Nuestra Señora of La Candelaria.

in a high location of Las Cuestas; **Parochial House** and an **old Cemetery**, also in the high part; and **Saint Antonio's Church**, built in 1959; all this in Tías.

Adding more: **Madalena Church**, 1978, in Masdache; **Church of the Virgin Nuestra Señora del Carmen** in Puerto del Carmen, built in 1890; and **Molino** in Mácher.

Puerto del Carmen beaches.

Testeyna Mountain surrounded by vineyards in La Geria.

Surroundings. Limited with San Bartolomé and Tinajo from the north; Yaiza from the west; and the sea from the south. The basic elements to highlight regarding the relief are: The La Geria, in the oriental part of the municipality, covered area by recent volcanic eruptions materials and with an excellent agricultural utilization. The alignment of volcanoes of *Montaña Blanca, Tersa, Bermeja, Conil, Tegoyo, Gaida* and *Guardilama*. And from here, the hillsides descend smoothly to the coastal beaches. The Puerto del Carmen area is composed of a beach chain; *Guasimeta, Hoyas Hondas, Los Pocillos, Playas Blanca*, and *Cangrejo* with the *Tiñosa* fishing port, already pointed out by Torriani in his map. Nowadays an urbanization of several kilometers of extension form that area, being the bigger of the island.

Useful information.

City council: Libertad street 36. 35573 Tías.
Tel.: 83 36 19 - 83 35 57

Hermitage of Mácher

YAIZA

History. In the *Rubicón* area, the plains in the south of Femés between Playa Blanca and *Punta Papagayo* (the first franc-Norman establishment) was built. The first bishopric was created by Pope Benedicto XIII, staying until it was transferred to Gran Canaria. However, the inhospitable of the place and the lack of defence forced the scarce inhabitants to move to Femés, located on high and more to the interior. During centuries the remains of the city-castle and the hermitage-cathedral were ignored and forgotten. In 1631, the bishop Cámara y Muga prepared the transfer of the image and the cult of Saint Marcial to Femés. The ruins have been completely abandoned after some excavations for studying. The last one was abandoned in 1986, and it is difficult to find now. In 1741, the Military Commandant of Canary ordered to build the *Aguila* or *Las Coloradas* tower fort, according to a project of the engineer Carlos de Lisle. Destroyed later on, it was reformed in Carlos III' command in 1769. Yaiza was being formed as an agricultural small town that took advantage of the wide plains of western sector. In 1699 their hermitage was built as a parish in September of 1728. Starting from 1730 it suffered the uncertainties of the volcanoes of Timanfaya area even fearing the destruction of the town. So it was abandoned in the moments of more danger. Fermés had 218 inhabitants in 1860, but the population was increasing up to 3.800 in 1920. Later it diminished until drastically it was absorbed by Yaiza in 1952.

General information. A population with about 7,000 inhabitants. It occupies 211'8 sq. km extension. The capital has 192 m altitude. Population's entities that depends on Yaiza are: Las Breñas, Femés, El Golfo, Playa Blanca, Uga, La Hoya, Playa Quemada, Cortijo Viejo, La Degollada, La Geria, Maciot, and Puerto Calero.

The economy is based fundamentally on the tourism, concentrated in Playa Blanca and Timanfaya.

The most important festivities are: The Virgin of Los Remedios, in September and Saint Marcial on July 7th.

Patrimony:

Nuestra Señora de la Caridad Hermitage (La Geria). Building from the XVII century, possesses a painting of the Virgin of La Caridad. The handmade roof highlights.

Parish of Nuestra Señora de los Remedios (Yaiza). The first hermitage was built in 1699 and it possibly belongs together with one of the naves of the present time. Later on, the hermitage was been reformed

Cemetery of Femés.

Calero Port.

Goats in Los Ajaches.

until what we see today. It has a plan with irregular geometry formed by a main nave with a biggest Altar, and two smaller in the side are located. In the main part of the temple there are the biggest Chapel and two lateral sacristies. The naves and lateral chapels are separated by circular columns with octagonal base. A gutter of basaltic stone whose capital and arch are made with clearer color calcareous stone. The arches are half point with polygonal profile. In the interior we can contemplate a central altarpiece and paintings located aside.

Church of Saint Martial (Femés). It was built at the beginning of the XVII century and change into parish in 1818. In the interior it has curious collars that adorn the gutters of the columns and arcades. A museum of naval scale models can be visited to contemplate several altarpieces, and a copy of the patron saint image from the XVIII century. The original image was destroyed by a fire.

Adding more: the **Archaeological area of the Rudicón**; **Natal house of Benito Pérez Galdós** (Fermés); **Tower of El Aguila** (Playa Blanca); **Isaac Viera Cultural Center**, the **School**, **Restaurant and "La Era" gardens**, and the **House of Benito Pérez Armas**, Remedios square, today a Culture House in Yaiza. Open to the public from Monday to Friday from 10 to 13 h. and from 16 to 19 h.

Surroundings. It occupies the south end
of the island, limiting to the north with Tinajo and to the east with Tías. The other limits are a quite varied coastal perimeter. The western sector of this perimeter is formed by the *malpaís* of *Timanfaya*, with the peculiarities of the lagoon of *Los Clicos* in the Golfo. It is called this way because in a past, there was this shellfish in its waters, and the *Hervideros*, group of caves and *bufaderos* where the water of the sea when penetrating seems to boil with the force of the waves. Just when the lava finishes, the lagoon of the *Janubio* and

the impressive salt flats open up. A coast of low cliffs continue until *Pechiguera* point. From here until *Papagayo* point. Beaches of white sand are inserted ending with cliffs of the east coast in the spurs of massif of *Los Ajaches*. This massif dominates the municipality and it is surround by big valleys as *Fena* and *Femés,* as well as those that come to the east cost. The north part is occupied by the cones and lava of the historical eruptions described thoroughly already.

About the urban areas, besides Yaiza and Femés, it is necessary to highlight,: Uga, small town of rural housings that has been reconstructed partly on the recent lava; and Playa Blanca, an old village of fishermen become into another tourist emporium, with fishermen's wharf, and commercial, sport and communication port with Fuerteventura.

Useful information.

City council: Los Remedios square. 35.570 Yaiza.
Tel.: 83 01 02   Fax: 83 00 35
Yaiza Gallery: General highway, 3. Open daily from 17 to 19 h., except Sundays. Tel.: 83 01 99
Local library: 83 02 75
Police Station: 83 01 07

BEACHES

The coast longitude has approximately 195 km. plus 55 kms (pertains to the islets) make a total of 250 km. distributed as follows: 157 km. between high and low cliffs; 62 km. between low costs and gravel beaches; and 30 km. with sand beaches, out of 10 km. are artificial ones.

In this distance 99 beaches are located in Lanzarote, 9 in La Graciosa and one in Alegranza. Only 56 are considered useful for tourist-recreational purposes. 33 are small, 15 medium and 8 big size. Most of then are fine sand beaches, others thick sand beaches, and some pebble and sand beaches. The white-golden color is the dominant one, followed by brown or toasted, and dark or black.

The followings are the most outstanding beaches (from Arrecife toward the north):

Reducto Beach: 470 m. longitude with artificial golden sand beach located in Arrecife. The access is easy.

Bastian Beach and Cucharas Beach: With 360 m. and 600 m. longitude respectively with artificial golden sand beaches located in Costa Teguise urbanization. The access is easy from the urban walk that surrounds them. It is advisable certain caution in windy days and to keep in mind the depth.

Caletón Blanco Beach: Beautiful 500 m white sand beach located close to Orzola. Although the access is easy, it must be done in some specific vehicle.

The whole coast of this area is configured in the *malpais* of La Corona. It is a low, rocky coast, with some incoming of calcareous materials that give place to these singular beaches of great contrast with a volcanic environment. They are notably inserted and it continues in a line of white dunes toward the interior.

The specific vegetation of the dunes are made up of *balancones* (Traganum Moquinii), *salados* (Arthrocnemum Fruticosum), *saladillos* (atriplex glauca), *orquídeas del desierto* (cistanche phelipaea), *spurge*, among others. Great quantity of *tabaibas dulce* (sweet Auphorbia), and important lichens communities are found among the volcanic rocks.

Risco Beach: with 915 m. longitude. Wild beach of fine and brown color beach in the bottom of *Riscos* of *Famara*. The access is complicated since it needs to be reached by ship from Orzola, Caleta de Famara or Caleta del Sebo in La Graciosa. Or it can be reached after a beautiful walk of about one hour through the way to *Guinate* which it goes down to the cliff of *Famara*. Keep in mind the hard climbing when going back through the same road. Although a beautiful and solitary beach is the recompense. Still not very advisable when windy days. We advise you to go prepare for the day; food, water, hat, etc.

This beach has important values to the landscaping, historical surroundings, with the *salinas* of *El Río*, fountain of *Gusa*, a prehistoric locations; botani-

Las Cucharas beach.

Caletón Blanco beach.

Risco beach.

Famara beach.

Santa Sport beach.

cal, with great variety and typical plants of sandbanks, salt-pit, swamps, and rocky cliffs; ornithological, *limícolas* birds and the typical predators of Lanzarote can be observed flying over the cliff.

Famara Beach: 2.800 m. longitude. Beach of fine sand and brown color, located in the bottom of the cliff of the same name. The access must be by some means of locomotion. When windy days is not advisable. It presents some danger due to the continuous surf. In the center of the beach there are some sunken ship remains.

The beginning of the beach is occupied by a line up of rounded rocks from a basaltic origin. Dunes are observed behind the beach and they are anchored in big *balancones* that can reach two meters long. They conform a characteristic landscape.

Santa Sport Beach: 940 m. long artificial beach next to the sport facilities of Santa Sport. The access is easy. This beach belongs to a small lake formed artificially when having blocked the natural water way through *El Río*, a sea arm that separates *La Isleta*.

Other beaches: **Mujeres, Pozo, Cera, Papagayo, Caleta del Congrio** and **Puerto Muelas.** They are a group of calcareous nature, clean, and golden sand beaches located to the south of the island with about 105 and 415 m. long. They are separated to each other by high promontories. Some in enclosed creek, so they are good for windy days. The access is easy

Pozo beach, Cera beach, and Mujeres beach.

Papagayo beach.

Blanca beach.

La Concha beach.

but it must be reached by some means of locomotion and from Playa Blanca's town.

The dominant vegetation is a heath of furzes and *bruscas*. These typical communities of sandbanks are located behind the beach.

Blanca Beach and Pocillos Beach: golden sand beaches with 1060 m and 1275 m. long respectively. Located in Puerto del Carmen. They have easy access but not very advisable when windy days. The accumulated sands, as much in the beaches as behind the beach are eolic origin and they possibly come from the *jable* of *Famara*. Behind Pocillos beach are two ponds which communicate directly with the sea.

The beaches are surrounded by a marine walk and they are integrated totally in the town.

Las Conchas Beach: this beach is located in the west coast of La Graciosa island, next to the volcanic cone of *Montaña Bermeja*. It is a white sand beach of about 500 m. long. It extends toward the interior of a group of dunes fed by the beach sands. The access should be on foot or by bicycle from Caleta del Sebo, in a forty five minutes beautiful walk crossing the isle. It is worthwhile to contemplate this half wild place, the contrasts of colors among the red volcano, the black rock, and the white sand.

Bibliography and Cartography.

The acquired knowledge on the island is given by different procedures which we can summarize mainly in two: one documentary and other direct. The direct information is the result of our field works on the spot, by interviewing to expert people from the island or, for our own interpretation through photographic material. The documentary information can be published or not. But the one published is for the traveller more easy of getting.

With the edition of this work we had preferred to pick up the biggest quantity of information of Lanzarote. But it is evident that for content and space reasons the book is only a synthesis of all the collected information. We suppose that certain topics will bring the reader interest. And for that we think it is interesting to give a relationship of books, classified by content, to enlarge your knowledge on the island.

We also want to thank the authors of these books, for their effort and dedication. This publication had not been possible without them. Most of the cited books have been good as bibliographical documents for the writing of our work.

General subjects:
- "*Atlas Básico de Canarias*". Canaria Interinsular Editorial. Santa Cruz de Tenerife. 1.980

- F. JAVIER GONZALEZ, PILAR MORIN y J. EZEQUIEL ACOSTA: "*La Graciosa*". Insular council town of Lanzarote. 1.996
- RAIMUNDO RODRIGUEZ y RAFAEL PAREDES: "*Fuerteventura*". Guías y Mapas RAI•MUNDO. 1.993
- Art, Culture and Tourism Centers. Insular council town of Lanzarote.

Geology:
- ARAÑA V. Y CARRACEDO J.: "*Los Volcanes de las Islas Canarias II, Lanzarote y Fuerteventura*". Editorial Rueda. Madrid. 1.979.
- OEDEX: "*Estudio de la Dinámica Litoral en la Costa de las Islas Canarias*". Studies and Experimentation Center of Ports and Coasts. MOPU. 1.986.
- BRAVO, T.: " *El volcán y el malpaís de La Corona. La Cueva de los Verdes y Los Jameos*". Insular council town publ. of Lanzarote, Arrecife. 1.964.
- FUSTER, J.M., FERNANDEZ, S., SAGREDO, J.: "*Geología y Vulcanología de las Islas Canarias, Lanzarote*". C.S.I.C., Madrid. 1.968.
- RUMEU, A. y ARAÑA, V.: "*Diario pormenorizado de la erupción volcánica de Lanzarote en 1.824*". An. Est. Atlánticos, 28. 1.982.
- CARRACEDO, J.C. y RODRÍGUEZ BADIOLA, E.: "*Lanzarote, la erupción de 1.730*".
- ORTIZ, R.: "*Guía Vulcanológica de Lanzarote*". C.S.I.C.
- ROBERTO SCANDONE Y MASSIMO CORTINI. *Revista Investigación y Ciencia*. Temas 8. (Investigation and Science Magazine. Chapter 8).

Ecology:
- ORTUÑO F. Y CEBALLOS L.: "*Vegetación y Flora de Las Canarias Occidentales*". Ministry of Agriculture. Madrid. 1.951.
- KUNKEL G.: "*Arboles y Arbustos de las Islas Canarias*". Edirca S.A. Las Palmas de Gran Canaria. 1.981.
- FONT TULLOT, I.: "*El Tiempo Atmosférico en las Islas Canarias*". National Meteorological Service Publications. Madrid. 1.956.
- ERIKSSON, O.; HANSEN A. y SUNDING, P.: "Flora of Macaronesia". Botanical Garden and Museum, University of Oslo. Norway. 1.979.
- PIZARRO, M.: "*Peces de Fuerteventura*". Government of Canary. Agriculture and Fishing Council Office. 1.985.

- CARRASCO, A.: *"Flora y Vegetación singular de Lanzarote".*
- BELTRAN, W.: *"Paraje Natural Barranco de Tenegüime".*

History, Art, Archaeology, Language:

- SUAREZ ACOSTA, J.J., RODRIGUEZ LORENZO, F. y QUINTERO PADRON, C.L.: "Conquista y Colonización". Canary Popular Culture Center.
- ARCO AGUILAR, Mª. C. y NAVARRO MEDEROS, J. F.: "Los Aborígenes".
- CABRERA PEREZ, J.C.: "Lanzarote y los Majos". Canary Popular Culture Center.
- MARTIN HORMIGA, A. F. y PERDONO, M. A.: "José Ramírez y César Manrique". Servicio de Publicaciones del Cabildo de Lanzarote.
- FRANCISCO PEREZ SAAVEDRA. "Lanzarote". Canary Popular Culture Center. 1.985
- ALBERTO LUENGO Y CIPRIANO MARIN: "El Jardín de la Sal". 1.994

Costumbres:

- Varios autores.: "Juegos deportivos tradicionales". Canary Popular Culture Center.
- CABRERA, B.: "El folklore de Lanzarote". Canary Popular Culture Center.
- HERNANDEZ DELGADO, F. y RODRIGUEZ ARMAS, M. D.: "La cocina de Lanzarote". Ayuntamiento de Teguise. Canary Popular Culture Center.

Mapas.

- Mapas Geológico de España (1:50.000 - 4 hojas). Instituto Geológico y Minero de España. C.S.I.C.
- Cartografía militar de España (Serie L, 1:50.000 - 5 hojas; Serie C, 1:100.000 - 2 hojas). Servicio Geográfico del Ejército.
- Cabildo Insular de Lanzarote (1:200.000).
- Instituto Hidrográfico de la Marina (1:50.000 - 4 hojas).
- Mapas RAI ● MUNDO (1:62.500 - 1 hoja). Mapa sobre base fotográfica a todo color.
- Mapas RAI ● MUNDO. Fotografía aérea (1:62.500 - 1 hoja, plastificado).

Famara

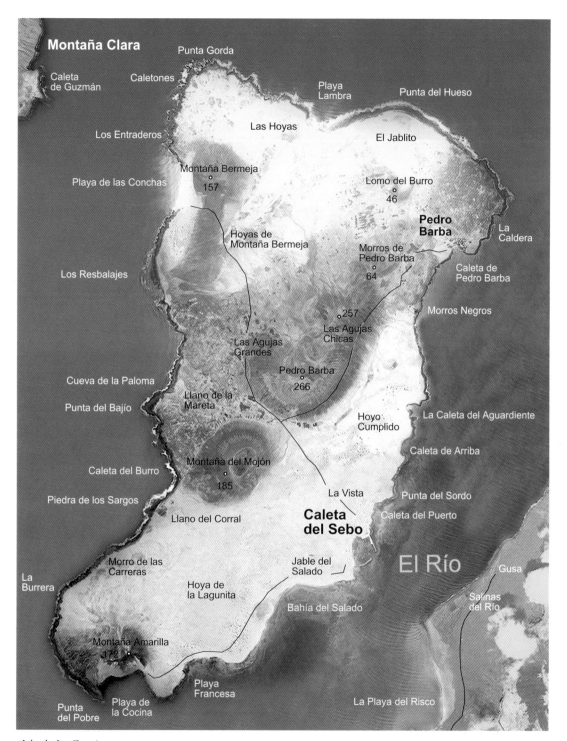

Isla de La Graciosa

Orzola

Punta Mujeres

Arrieta

Costa Teguise

HARIA

Tahiche

Ye

TEGUISE

El Río

Famara

LA GRACIOSA

Soo

La Isleta

ARRECIFE

SAN BARTOLOME

Aeropuerto

TIAS

Puerto del Carmen

Puerto Calero

TIMANFAYA

YAIZA

Femés

Punta de Papagayo

Playa Blanca

El Golfo

Laguna de Janubio

Punta de Pechiguera